"As always with Simon's teaching, this book combines biblical exposition, practical application, and amusing and reflective anecdotes. It helpfully unpacks God's passion for justice, a passion shared by Tearfund in our relief and development work with the world's poorest people. Simon is honest about his own struggles with feelings of guilt and condemnation in the face of the scale of global poverty and injustice, but he inspires his readers to respond with compassion, practical action, and service. I highly recommend it."

— Joanna Watson, Tearfund's Advocacy Advisor

"These short yet significant meditations refreshed my passion and commitment to see God's loving heart shared through the actions and reactions I take with those around me. If you want to be inspired, challenged and motivated to live out the love of God as a follower of Jesus, then this is the book for you too."

— Joseph Steinberg, CMS Director

"Simon's compelling exploration of justice and mercy is rich fare indeed. It is a feast of truth, served up in tenderness; it challenges and chastens, it prods and provokes. You will be nourished and satisfied by it, but it will recall forgotten passions and purpose – read it prepared to live differently."

— Anita Cleverly, Ask Prayer Network, Senior Leadership Team, St Aldates Oxford

"In Simon Ponsonby the church has found an eloquent, theological and biblical writer, persuasive in his conviction that a life seeking holiness and more of the Spirit will also always be a life passionately concerned with justice and mercy."

— Dr Stephen Backhouse, Tutor in Social and Political Theology, St Mellitus College

Loving Mercy

How to serve a tender-hearted Saviour

Simon Ponsonby

MONARCH
BOOKS

Oxford, UK & Grand Rapids, Michigan, USA

First published in the UK in 2012 by Monarch Books
(a publishing imprint of Lion Hudson plc)
Wilkinson House, Jordan Hill Road, Oxford OX2 8DR, England
Tel: +44 (0)1865 302750 Fax: +44 (0)1865 302757
Email: monarch@lionhudson.com
www.lionhudson.com

ISBN 978 0 85721 251 1 (print)
ISBN 978 0 85721 343 3 (Kindle)
ISBN 978 0 85721 344 0 (epub)

Distributed by:
UK: Marston Book Services, PO Box 269, Abingdon, Oxon, OX14 4YN
USA: Kregel Publications, PO Box 2607, Grand Rapids, Michigan 49501

British Library Cataloguing Data
A catalogue record for this book is available from the British Library.

Printed and bound in the UK by MPG Books.

For Tiffany
remplie de tendresse

Also by Simon Ponsonby:

More

God Inside Out

The Pursuit of the Holy

The Lamb Wins

Now to Him

Contents

Foreword

One day a homeless lady approached a vicar who was visibly flustered and stressed. She needed help, but he was simply too busy, so he promised to pray for her and then carried on his way. That lady wrote the following poem and gave it to a local Shelter officer:

> I was hungry,
> And you formed a humanities group to discuss my hunger.
> I was imprisoned,
> And you crept off quietly to your chapel and prayed for
>   my release.
> I was naked,
> And in your mind you debated the morality of my appearance.
> I was sick,
> And you knelt and thanked God for your health.
> I was homeless,
> And you preached a sermon on the spiritual shelter of the
>   love of God.
> I was lonely,
> And you left me alone to pray for me.
> You seem so holy, so close to God
> But I am still very hungry – and lonely – and cold.

I find the above story very challenging, and even guilt-inducing. I empathize fully with the beleaguered vicar, having been in similar situations myself on countless occasions, albeit in my very different context of working for a decade in the world's fourth poorest nation, Burundi. And I think we all feel helpless and overwhelmed sometimes at the countless needs that bombard us either directly or on the news.

In any case, what you have before you is a fantastic resource that steers clear of the guilt trips while retaining a challenging thrust to embrace a costly engagement with God's heart for his world.

In *Loving Mercy* we are presented with rigorous biblical backing and analytical thinking coupled with accessible anecdotes and quotes that draw us closer to our "tender-hearted Saviour". Simon is not an ivory tower theologian writing in a theoretical vacuum; rather he is a deeply rooted passionate practitioner who, as both theologian and pastor, wants to share what he has gleaned from the depths for the benefit of the body of Christ.

Edmund Burke once declared: "All that it takes for evil to prosper is for righteous people to do nothing." As followers of Christ, we have both the enormous privilege and the awesome responsibility to *do* something, to be both hearers and doers, which is what Simon is longing for us to embrace through his latest book. (As we are reminded in Luke 12:48 "Everyone to whom much was given, of him much will be required.") The church in some quarters (by no means everywhere) is a slumbering giant with extraordinary potential to change the world, if we work together in unity and purpose to enact our God-given mandate as ministers of mercy.

So you want something challenging, biblically rooted, relevant, and practical? This book could, by God's grace, provide just the shaking and stirring you need to ramp things up in your own life and community. And ultimately, you will be left asking the painfully searching question: will I love the truth enough to live it?

Simon Guillebaud, Founder of Great Lakes Outreach

Who Wants to Be a Millionaire?

My first book *More* was about how we can be filled with the Holy Spirit. Later I wrote a less popular book (in terms of sales figures) called *The Pursuit of the Holy* that was about how I could be more Christ-like. This current book on justice and mercy flows out of the years of study and reflection and pursuit of how to be filled with the Spirit and how to be more like Jesus.

What does the Spirit-filled life look like? Living justly and mercifully. What does the sanctified life look like? Living justly and mercifully. The Spirit-filled and sanctified life look like a life lived, not inwardly but outwardly, not wanting more for me but wanting more for others, not desiring mere personal transformation but social transformation. The Spirit-filled, Christ-like church will have her affections stirred for God and all that stirs God's affections: the kingdom on earth as it is in heaven, a rule of righteousness, a kind kingdom. Jesus once said of Mary who anointed him with nard before his death, "She has done what she could" (Mark 14:8). That's all he asks of us – to do what we can – for him and for the world he so loves.

A good friend of mine was invited to speak at a conference. He very quickly felt awkward as every message was on prosperity doctrine and how God wanted all believers to be rich, explaining the steps of faith and declaration that would bring in the big bucks. My pal, known for his ministry to the poor in India, was surprised to be in such company, but assumed God had orchestrated it and that the hosts knew him and the burden of his message. So when it came time for him to speak, he duly delivered a talk on his favourite theme, from James 2, namely God's heart for the poor and the church's need to have God's heart. He didn't find delivering the sermon easy, sensing resistance in the room to his theme. Justice and mercy were not the dish of the day.

When he finished and sat down to stunned silence, it seemed as if tumbleweed was rolling in front of him. The host, a Canadian with a Texan accent, stood and spoke. He began by saying he had found the sermon difficult and had not understood what it was about. My friend thought, "Well, at least that's honest and humble." But what the host went on to say made my friend sit up. He continued: "I struggled with what our brother was saying today until God gave me revelation." My friend was all ears, thinking that perhaps God had brought him here just for this, bringing a revelation of his heart to these men.

It was not to be. The compère, standing with microphone to mouth, legs set apart in dominant posture, arm rotating in wide circles like a windmill, and index finger pointing at the people on each completed iteration, slowly screamed out these words at fever pitch:

You –

can –

all –

be –

millionaires!

Instantly the crowd leapt from their seats, began shouting and cheering and running to the front, throwing their credit cards and their money on the stage – believing they were sowing, and so naturally they would reap! In an instant the atmosphere changed from soporific indifference to my friend's message on mercy, to the pulsing electricity of a golden-calf party. My friend bowed his head, fought back the tears, rose from his seat and walked out. Giddy with the thought that soon they might all be millionaires, no one noticed him leave. But I am quite sure that God looked at my friend and smiled, even while those with dollar signs in their hearts were making him wince.

Jesus defined his ministry by saying the Spirit was upon him to preach good news to the poor, to bind up the broken hearted, give sight to the blind and release for the captives, and proclaim the year of the Lord's favour. In this book I want to think about exactly who are the poor, the broken, the blind and the captives, and to consider how Christ through us is bringing them favour. Can we find God's heart for the lost, the last, and the least?

The well-known Canadian author and teacher Guy Chevreau tells how he stopped at a traffic light in Toronto to talk to a homeless guy. The man had a grubby cardboard sign, and on it was written: "Homeless and Hungry, Broke and Broken – please help. God Bless." Guy couldn't get this man's sign out of his head – or his heart. You see, life *with* the Holy Spirit is to care for those in that hurting place who live life *without* the Holy Spirit: the homeless and hungry, the broke and broken. And we the church are called, not to prosperity but to mercy; to grace the poor; not to get full but to feed the hungry; not to buy a holiday home but to see the homeless homed; not to go to health spas to get our toenails tidied but to heal the broken.

The Hollywood blockbuster *Slumdog Millionaire* follows the journey of an Indian boy who survives in the slums of Mumbai and eventually escapes the depravity and poverty by winning a fortune as a contestant on a TV quiz show. It's a story of hope in despair. But very few really get lucky and get out. Most don't stand a chance. We may all have watched the movie – but were we moved by it? And how were we moved? To do what? What does the incarnation tell us? What does the Spirit provoke in us?

Some who are reading this book have the creative, productive business skills to make a million. Do it. Missions work costs millions. But live by Methodist founder John Wesley's motto: "Make all you can, save all you can, give all you can." Others reading this are called to be downwardly mobile, not lovers of money but lovers of the needy, seeking out where slumdogs sleep, and sharing the gospel, sharing our daily bread, sharing ourselves, sharing God.

Chapter 1

Second Conversion

I have a dream that my four little children will one day live in a nation where they will not be judged by the color of their skin but by the content of their character.[1]
Martin Luther King

The prejudice seen by Martin Luther King as he campaigned for justice with the US Civil Rights movement is sadly far from unique, yet it poses one of the greatest obstacles to living out justice and mercy. We hear of institutional prejudice like that encountered by King, and of individual moments of prejudice, such as that experienced by Mahatma Gandhi when he was turned away by an usher from a church in London as a student – despite having been drawn to the lack of prejudice in the Jesus he had read about in the Gospels. Gandhi, as history records, returned to India, and despite his best efforts for peace, oversaw the partitioning into India and Pakistan amid a tidal wave of bloodshed. How different might that continent look, how different might history be, had that dear man been shown the way to Jesus rather than shown the door.

In the face of deep racial prejudice, Nelson Mandela powerfully observed in *Long Walk to Freedom* that "No one is born hating another person because of the colour of his skin, or his background, or his religion. People must learn to hate, and if

1   http://www.americanrhetoric.com/speeches/mlkihaveadream.htm

they can learn to hate, they can be taught to love, for love comes more naturally to the human heart than its opposite."

Proud and prejudiced

The apostle Peter had learned to hate the non-Jew. Even when already committed to following Christ and preaching the gospel, Peter had not yet let Jesus teach him to love the Gentiles. Yet where did he learn to hate?

Perhaps the oppressive brutal Roman occupation of his nation with its countless injustices against his own people had done this, following on as it did from a history of invasions and oppression under the Persians and the Greeks. Perhaps as a young boy he witnessed the 2,000 Jews crucified in Galilee, lining her streets with the blood and the death of his kith and kin.[2] Fear, even stretching to paranoia, regarding the Gentiles was by no means limited to Peter. There was no love lost between Israel and the other people groups, no trust – what nation had ever done right by them?! That's why Jesus was pressed hard when he said "love thy neighbour" (Mark 12:31 KJV) as to exactly who "my neighbour" was. Hearing it was a half-breed, a half-Jewish and half-Gentile Samaritan, would have been a traumatic thought to a Jew.

Perhaps Peter's prejudice also stemmed from the exclusive nature of his Judaism, inculcated since he was a toddler. He had grown up knowing that he was part of the people God had chosen from Abraham for his own possession, whose unique role was to be the priests of God to the world. They were "a peculiar people" whose rules and regulations enforced a strict distinction between them and all others. They were to be separate. This distinction was enforced on a daily – even momentary – basis through strict

2   Josephus records in *Jewish Antiquities* 7:295 that in 4 BC, 2,000 Jews were crucified in Galilee on the orders of Varus, Roman Legate of Syria, after a minor revolt.

rules of purity and separation. Merely entering the home of a Gentile was enough to make a Jew unclean (Acts 10:28), and one of the worst sins was marriage between Jew and Gentile.

Peter had a hard heart to Gentiles – especially Roman soldiers, their uniform ever the symbol of those who slew his Master. Many of us have learned to hate. Justice and mercy begin when we see people as we see ourselves – when they become us. Justice and mercy begin when the scales that blind our eyes to others fall away, when bigotry and prejudice are exorcized by the Spirit of God who so loved the world that he gave to us. It is a painful exchange for many of us – to embrace those we would much more readily exclude. But until the affections of Christ are our affections, God's work is incomplete in us. We are like the blind man whom Jesus enables to see, but who initially can see only men as trees walking (Mark 8:22–25). Many of us have yet to see our fellow men walking: we cannot see the people for the trees.

A revelation and a revolution

What does it take to overcome such entrenched prejudice and to experience the "second conversion" that Peter needed in order fully to take up his place in God's plans for the world?

We see in Acts 10 that God brought to Peter three visions, three voices and three visitors to shake him out of his prejudice.[3] The use of three is significant here – in Jewish idiom, to say something three times was a way of expressing it definitively, permanently, and unequivocally. When God revealed himself to Isaiah and to John in the Apocalypse, the angels cried "Holy, holy, holy" (Isaiah 6:3; Revelation 4:8). The threefold repeat signifies perfection. So a threefold vision, voice, and visitors is as clear-cut as it gets: God is speaking.

---

3   This conversion is also discussed by my close colleague Charlie Cleverly in his recent book *Epiphanies of the Ordinary*, Hodder, 2012.

God arrests Peter three times with a shocking vision (Acts 10:11–16) of many kinds of animals on a sheet with four corners. The four corners represent the four corners of the world (Revelation 7:1), and the animals were both those set apart as clean and those considered unclean under Jewish law and so excluded from Peter's diet. To Peter's astonishment, God accompanies this vision each time with the command "Kill and eat". Peter's response to the command is the same each time – he refuses to eat, saying "I have never eaten anything that is common or unclean." Yet God responds three times with the same answer: "What God has made clean, do not call common."

The attitude and instruction of Jesus on the law of Moses has occupied theologians for two millennia. On the one hand he declared that not a jot or tittle would disappear from it, and on the other hand he declared he had come to fulfil it. Jesus universalized and intensified the moral law of the Old Testament, as "murder" was made to include anger and "adultery" now included lust. The law which gave permission for divorce was upgraded and the grounds for divorce reduced. Jesus' use of the phrase, "You have heard that it was said… But I say to you…" (Matthew 5:21) not only intensified the demands of the law but applied it to all disciples, not just the Jews.

And yet it is also clear that Christ reapplied the ceremonial law, especially where it related to cleanliness, diet, and special religious days. It was this easing of religious observation that aroused the anger of the Pharisees. He shocked them by personally associating with religiously unclean people – including lepers, women, tax collectors, and prostitutes – and this made Jesus ritually unclean in their eyes. He avoided a direct obedience to the letter of the law by not stoning a woman caught in adultery. And he "worked" on the Sabbath in ways that the Scribes and Pharisees deemed to be law-breaking.

Peter had learned much from his Master, but the visions, voice and later the visitors would inaugurate a paradigm shift. Peter was already on a journey of transformation. He was staying (presumably out of necessity) at the house of a tanner. Now the tanner's was a profession, which, because of its association with dead animals, was regarded as ritually unclean. By staying at this house Peter was already unclean by association. Incrementally God was stretching his worldview and theology, and rewriting his mission. However, Peter would need to let go of his commitment to ceremonial law if he was to fulfil the Great Commission and the Great Commandment. You cannot love your neighbour as yourself if your ceremonial laws of cleanliness and diet keep you at a distance. Peter had received the Great Commission to "go and make disciples of all nations", and at Pentecost he had received the power to be a witness to Jesus in Jerusalem, Judea, Samaria, and the ends of the earth. But for that to be fulfilled, to go to the "Gentile" uttermost ends, there needed to be a great transformation of Peter's heart. He needed a new affection. We see in Acts 8 that Peter was already willing to evangelize at home in Judea – indeed even in Samaria, where Jews and Gentiles had intermarried – but up to this point, his prejudices had not allowed him to witness "to the ends of the earth". Peter's prejudice made it impossible for him to obey the Great Commission, and it would take an extraordinary revelation to get him to go.

We probably all carry prejudices, and many of us are not even aware of them. Perhaps deep down we may think we are superior; such a belief may be unarticulated but strongly held. That other people group over there, "them", we truly regard as inferior, be that through:

race	education
creed	sexuality
colour	shape or size
age	hair length or colour
class	fashion.
gender	

We categorize and condemn them as less than us because they are not like us.

There are many in the church today giddy for a revelation of God. They have the plain commands in Scripture and the Spirit's leading within, but they want extraordinary visions, voices, visitations. Maybe God will grant them their wish – and take them to the people they previously despised! Peter's extraordinary revelation in Acts 10 came about because his prejudice had caused a reluctance in him to obey the Great Commission and go to the Gentiles. Oswald Chambers rightly noted, "The best measure of a spiritual life is not its ecstasies but its obedience."

Who are you better than, in your own mind? We need to ask God to search our souls and expose the subtle but deeply held resentments, superior spirits, judgmentalism, and prejudices. We are prejudiced when we single out any particular group and categorize them as "all the same". This applies to any people group we look at and look down on generically! Homeless or homeowners? So-called Whites or non-whites? Poor or prosperous? The old or the young? Males or females? Working class or upper class? BMW or Volvo drivers? Blondes or peroxide blondes? Fat people or skinny people? People who live in suburbia or in caravans or in mansions. Poles or the Welsh or the English… prejudice knows no boundaries and infects us all.

A Welsh friend told me that she grew up in a culture that

taught that every time she crossed the Severn Bridge from Wales into England she should spit, in a kind of ancient curse on the English who for centuries had oppressed their neighbour. I grew up with an inchoate hatred for Germans, no doubt fuelled by two world wars in living memory and an avid interest in twentieth-century military history. Say "German" and I thought "Nazi". Use a German accent and all I could imagine was orders barked at prisoners in concentration camps. Not until I became a Christian leader did God begin to put his finger on this and expose it as prejudice, racism, hatred, and sin. I found a friend, a dear German lady who met regularly with me and listened, and prayed, and shared about her family's experience of the war and their response to Hitler. This dear woman by proxy accepted my repentance for hating her people. She helped me to walk in the opposite spirit. I bought German cars, sought out Germans as friends, and even hoisted a German flag in my study so that whenever I looked at it I could pray and bless Germans. And slowly, over time, God so changed my heart that now I even get excited when I hear a German accent and greet a German person.

The apostle Paul wrote: "God shows no partiality" (Romans 2:11) and "There is neither Jew nor Greek, there is neither slave nor free, there is no male and female, for you are all one in Christ Jesus" (Galatians 3:28). In Christ our barriers come down, our barricades are dismantled. In this way we are called to reflect the openness of Jesus, imitating his engagement with all parts of his society – from young to old, rich to poor, "good" to scandalous. He was a man for all peoples.

By contrast there is a strongly promoted missionary model known as the "homogenous principle" which describes effective mission as when you target your own people group and give your church a single monoculture! Middle-class white church, working-class church, youth church, Chinese congregation, Nigerian church… yes, it's all very pragmatic and effective, because it appeals to latent prejudices and people prefer to be with "their own type". But as pragmatic mission underpinned by prejudice it's fundamentally unbiblical and unchristian.

I recognize that in many churches there may be several different congregations and no one belongs to them all. In my own church we have a "family-orientated" congregation, a "twenties–forties" congregation and a "teens and twenties" student congregation. Each has its own flavour and style. However, it is important that each recognize they are part of a larger, wider, varying family, and that – through shared notices, shared leadership team, shared publicity, shared mission teams, integrated pastorates and joint events – we work hard to create a sense of belonging.

Prejudice is the great barrier to global mission

It is impossible to witness effectively to someone you are dismissive of, or who you think is inferior to you in some way. Such prejudice is a barrier to mission because it does not allow the love of God to be shown through us, and nor does it allow God's Spirit to use us.

I recall hearing an unforgettable story told by that saintly old American Pentecostal Bible teacher, Judson Cornwall. In the 1960s he received an invitation to speak at a renewal conference in Germany. Having lived through the war, and having seen friends and family suffer as a consequence, Cornwall had a deep-seated grudge against the Germans. Not that he was aware of it; but when he read the invitation he scrunched it up and threw it in the bin without even replying.

Remarkably, his wife emptied the bin, found the invitation, pressed it out and put it back on his desk! It haunted him for days as he shuffled it around. Finally, the Spirit won over his reluctant flesh, and he reluctantly agreed to go. Arriving in Germany, he was not relieved in his dis-ease as the conference centre turned out to be the former headquarters of the SS, Hitler's élite guard, which aroused all sorts of images and old hatreds in him! He spent the two days before the conference praying and fasting and preparing – and avoiding Germans.

On the first night of the conference he went down to speak, and instantly took umbrage at his translator, a somewhat stereotypical Aryan *Überfrau* – giant, buxom, blonde hair in bun. He disliked her, and he disliked even more hearing his voice translated into German. He spat out his sermon, so it was no surprise that it was badly delivered, badly received, and died a death. He returned to his room and decided to go back to America the very next day. Full of humiliation and emotion, he wept himself to sleep.

In the night he awoke to demons screaming in his mind: *"You don't belong here! You have no authority here! Go home!"* Experienced in spiritual warfare and deliverance, Cornwall recognized this attack, figured it was something to do with the demonic history of the SS in the building, and immediately rebuked the demons in Jesus' name before going back to sleep. Three times the demonic voices woke him; three times he rebuked them and they left. After the third time, he got up and asked God what was happening and why his prayers weren't sufficient and the demons kept returning. The Lord spoke immediately: "The demons are tormenting you because you really do not have any authority here. You have no authority because you do not love these people. Your authority to minister is related to your love for those you minister to. Now, you can go on hating these people, pack up and go home tomorrow; or you can let me love them through you."

Cornwall acknowledged his deep racism and prejudice. Too

embarrassed to go home, he confessed his sin and asked God to love through him the Germans he loathed. He knew he needed a miracle of grace. Immediately he was overwhelmed by the Spirit of God and filled with Christ's love for the Germans. Having spent two days avoiding Germans and refusing to eat with them, he could not wait for breakfast. He rushed downstairs to the queue for breakfast and greeted and hugged everyone in the food line. When he got to his translator from the night before, he gave her a big kiss and embraced her. Immediately she pulled back and barked: "You hate us!"

"No, no," he replied, "that was yesterday – today I love you."

Judson Cornwall preached that morning and the power of God was upon his words. At the end of the sermon, there was a huge line of people wanting to speak personally to him, something that he usually avoided; but he sensed God wanted him to be attentive to the people individually. One by one, people came and thanked him for helping them to forgive the Americans – whether because they had lost loved ones in combat against them or in the bombing raids. Cornwall saw that pain and resentment and prejudice cuts both ways... but that obedience to the Spirit of Christ heals historic hurts and unites us in the love of God.

Burying prejudice

Peter's vision took place at Simon the Tanner's house in Joppa, now Jaffa, the Mediterranean seaside port halfway along Israel's coast. Joppa is only mentioned a couple of times in the Bible, most infamously as the port from where Jonah set sail, fleeing from God, refusing to take the gospel to Nineveh. It is at Joppa that we see Jonah's prejudice against the Ninevites which leads to his disobedience, with all its unpleasant consequences of storms and stomachs.

Joppa thus represents to us a place of decision: whether or not we will obey God's call to overcome social and racial prejudices and take the gospel to former enemies. Jonah at Joppa disobeys God. But Peter at Joppa finally accepts a command to bury his prejudice concerning Gentiles, and he ministers to the Roman Cornelius. At Joppa Jonah broke ranks with God – prejudice got the better of him. At Joppa Peter broke through – God got the better of his prejudice! A knock at the door brings the three visitors from Cornelius, against Jewish custom but after Jesus' heart, and Peter welcomes the Gentile strangers into his room. He accompanies them to Cornelius's home where he shares the gospel of Christ with them. The Spirit falls, the whole family is saved, and so begins the great missionary expansion to the Gentile world.

Who is knocking at your door?

Chapter 2

Justice People

The just man justices...[4]
Gerard Manley Hopkins

Thousands of years ago God asked the question of our ancestor, "Where is your brother Abel?" And Cain, who had just slain him, replied: "Am I my brother's keeper?" God's unspoken answer was "Yes – you absolutely are!" And throughout humanity's history, whenever the same selfish protestation has arisen, God has cried, "Yes!"

Jesus summed up the whole law of God as "love the Lord your God with all your heart ... soul ... strength ... mind, and your neighbour as yourself" (Luke 10:27). Every religious soul knows that God deserves to be loved like that – with the totality of our being. But to love our neighbour like that? Surely that depends who the neighbour is... doesn't it?

Jesus answered that question with the parable of the Good Samaritan (Luke 10:30–35). Our neighbour is revealed to be *anyone* we see who needs our help. We love our neighbour if we put ourselves out on their account, and if we pay for their well-being. We fail the test if we walk on by, disregarding the plight of the neighbour, whether known or unknown, named or unnamed. We fail the test even if we are in a hurry to get to our place of worship. In fact, if we do not love our neighbour, we cannot love our God, and we had better not go to worship

---

4   From the poem "As Kingfishers Catch Fire" by Gerard Manley Hopkins.

because God won't be there for us. "When you failed the least of these, you failed me…" (Matthew 25:45, author's paraphrase).

Luke wanted to make the point in recording the parable that the Samaritan, who was Israel's historic despised enemy, was fulfilling the law of God by assisting a victim of abuse and robbery and going out of his way to help out; whereas the religious priest and Levite, those who were perceived as paragons of religious virtue, walked on by and in so doing walked away from God. Much that looks religious has little to do with righteousness.

The famed Swiss theologian Karl Barth often repeated the axiom "Your ethics are the test of your dogmatics." How you live in the world in relationship with others shows the quality of your beliefs. In the New Testament, James showed us that our deeds prove our doctrines (James 2:18). The flesh, under the guise of religion, often pulls us into an introspective and self-centred spirituality, and this can easily be baptized by Christian tradition, as the fear of religious contamination leads to separatism. And so Pharisees will not sit and eat with tax collectors or sinners: they pay their tithes yet neglect weightier matters of justice. Later on aspects of the monastic tradition will withdraw from society to pray and enjoy God; the mystic tradition will be given to navel-gazing in their pursuit of God, while Puritans and Pietists emphasize cultural separation. Evangelicals will await the Rapture, in the hope of leaving the world to go up in smoke, while Charismatics will get on yet another plane, increasing their carbon footprint, just to lie on yet another carpet for yet another cuddle from Jesus. How sorely we need to heed the wisdom of Charles Finney, that famous nineteenth-century American revivalist: "The great business of the church is to reform the world. If she doesn't engage in social reform, she grieves the Holy Spirit and hinders revival."[5]

---

5   Charles Finney, *Letters On Revivals: No. 23*, 21 January, 1846.

1. The mission of Jesus was marked by justice and mercy

Mrs Moore in E. M. Forster's *A Passage to India* remarked, "Poor little talkative Christianity."[6] How sadly true this often is of the church, though it was never true of Christ. As John Oswalt wrote, "Will the Servant / Messiah simply hurl words at the poor? No…."[7] Jesus acted to make a difference. Matthew, quoting Isaiah, said of Jesus: "He will proclaim justice to the Gentiles" and will "bring justice to victory" (Matthew 12:18–20). Justice is at the heart of the so-called Messianic Manifesto, and so the Spirit was upon him to "bring good news to the poor … to bind up the brokenhearted, to proclaim liberty to the captives, and the opening of the prison to those who are bound," and to proclaim the Jubilee, the "year of the Lord's favour" when all debt is to be cancelled (Isaiah 61:1–2; also Luke 4:18–19).

We dare not overspiritualize these statements of Jesus' ministry – they are robust practical acts of justice and mercy. Jesus fed the hungry; Jesus touched the leper; Jesus restored the prostitute; Jesus absolved the sinners; Jesus raised the dead son of a poor lone widow; Jesus overthrew the tables and whipped the rip-you-off money changers out of the temple; Jesus told the rich man salvation was found in selling and giving all he had to the poor; Jesus warned us that the criteria on judgment day for inclusion in his eternal kingdom included whether we had clothed the naked, fed the hungry, and visited the prisoner.

Jesus' miracles are not simply demonstrations of power per se, they are demonstrations of the justice, mercy, compassion, forgiveness, restoration, and acceptance of God – they reveal his heart, not just his hand; his passion, not just his power. John

---

6   E. M. Forster, *A Passage to India*, p. 139.
7   John Oswalt, Isaiah 40–66, *New International Commentary on the Old Testament* p. 565.

Nolland wrote, "Jesus is no social reformer, and does not address himself in any fundamental way to the political structure of the world, but he is deeply concerned with the literal, physical needs of men as with their spiritual needs."[8]

Peter summarizes Jesus' ministry with the beautiful phrase, "he went about doing good" (Acts10:38). Jesus established a kingdom of justice, and it was a kingdom of kindness. Jesus bought our justification by satisfying God's just wrath on our sin. Jesus will return as the just judge – to rid the world finally and fully of all evil and to establish an eternal heaven on earth, ordered by justice.

2. The early church was noted for justice and mercy

The German martyr Dietrich Bonhoeffer constructed a simple but profound theology: Christ at the centre of the church, church at the centre of the world. The Christ who is at this epicentre is Christ *pro nobis* – the man for us, the man for others. And Bonhoeffer certainly practised what he preached. The apostles preached justification by grace through faith alone (Ephesians 2:8) and they also preached that faith produces good works – (Ephesians 2:10; James 2:17). The truly justified act justly. Justice reveals the justified.

When Jesus ascended and sent his Spirit at Pentecost, it was not merely for us to feel a sense of "wow" but rather to feel God's heart for the world, a sense of "woe" and the compulsion to go and further the mission of Christ, to proclaim and perform the works of the kingdom. The Spirit that rested on Jesus was the Spirit of God, a spirit of justice and by filling all in the same way – old men and young, male and female, slave and free – God

---

8   John Nolland, Luke 1–9:20, *Word Biblical Commentary*, p. 197.

powerfully demonstrates a new equality as social differences that had often become social injustices began to be removed. Today, we simply cannot comprehend how radical the early church, was, how counter-cultural. She was persecuted by both devout Jew and pagan Roman precisely because of her revolutionary ethics of justice seen in equality. In a culture dominated by sexism, racism, and oppression Paul heralded the egalitarian revolution: in Christ there was to be no racial, classist, or gender-based distinction, because all were now one (Galatians 3:28).

Following its master, the early church became a form of social services – not just healing the sick but distributing its wealth so that none had need, providing "daily" food for widows (Acts 6:1). When Paul was converted and set apart as apostle to the Gentiles, the only thing the Jerusalem fathers asked him to do was to "remember the poor", the very thing Paul says he was keen to do. James tells us that the mark of the church is that both poor and rich are to be treated the same – indeed, partiality toward the wealthy is a sin that God will judge (James 2). Writing to Timothy, Paul lists a catalogue of sins, which includes "enslavers" – those who take others into slavery (1 Timothy 1:10). To have 26 million slaves in the world today is a sin and a stain on humanity. Paul prophetically tells Philemon to welcome his runaway slave as "a brother", and tradition records that Onesimus later became a bishop!

3. The Spirit rests on those committed to justice and mercy

It is a tragic fact that not all that goes by the name of Christianity has looked like Christ. Not all who claim to be justified have acted with justice. Not all who have received Christ's mercy have been merciful.

But where people have been filled with the Spirit of God, faithfully following the Son of God, obeying the Word of God and feeling the heart of God, the presence of grace, justice and mercy has been marked. This can be seen in the way the medieval church offered provision to the poor, hospitality to travellers, shelter for the vulnerable, and hospitals for pilgrims and lepers alike.

The church has a long history of providing for those in need, and such mercy stands out. In Mother Teresa, who spent her life caring for the sick and poor on the streets of Calcutta, continuing her work in the face of hardship and opposition, the journalist Malcolm Muggeridge was able to glimpse Christ. For Muggeridge, Mother Teresa's love and her choice to serve Christ through the poor and vulnerable stood out as uncommon – a level of sacrifice not often seen in our world. Such compassion continues to be lived out by charities and aid agencies ranging from the Red Cross to Viva International, and from Tearfund to Betel, which were prompted by Christ's call to justice and mercy. It is hard to name an aid agency that does not have Christian roots. The Spirit has led Christians throughout the centuries to pioneer change in society, championing campaigns as varied as the socialist movement, the feminist movement and the campaign for the abolition of slavery. "Since we are surrounded by so great a cloud of witnesses, let us also lay aside every weight, and sin which clings so closely, and let us run with endurance the race that is set before us" (Hebrews 12:1). We are filled with this same Spirit of God – so let us also pursue justice and mercy with such commitment.

Give a dog a bone

Some years ago I was in my car about six miles from my home when I saw a small black dog with a red collar and a cloverleaf dog-tag, running scared through the traffic. Being a dog lover, I was concerned and I wanted to get out and help it, but the traffic was moving, so I simply sent up a prayer and hoped that it knew its way home. Later that day, a further three miles away, I drove past the same dog, now looking haunted and still running scared. This time I stopped the car and ran after it, realizing it was lost and separated from its owner. But it ran off. I remained concerned about that dog and prayed for the next few days for it. Remarkably, five days later, I was walking my own dog around my parish, and I saw the same black dog, red collar, cloverleaf tag. This time it was skinny, hungry, its coat in bad shape, and it was eating garbage at the bins. It looked at me and then scarpered. I ran after it, calling to a group of lads to help me catch it, but it got away, thinking me foe not friend. I was gutted, and a deep sadness filled my emotions.

Then I sensed the Lord speak to me, one of those rare but unforgettable moments. "My son, you feel compassion for this hurting dog, alone, afraid, hungry, harassed and helpless, separated from its master. I am hurting for the world full of millions and millions of lost, hungry people – afraid, mistreated, feeding off filth, separated from me, their Master."

Jesus once said, "Which one of you who has a sheep [or a dog!], if it falls into a pit on the Sabbath, will not take hold of it and lift it out? Of how much more value is a man than a sheep!" (Matthew 12:11–12).

Chapter 3

Justice God

"Which is justice? Which is the thief?" [9]
William Shakespeare

Over a million children are trafficked each year. The industry is worth $12 billion dollars to the black market. I once heard of a girl who was sold into slavery by her parents, who were poor. She became a sex slave. An aid agency worker asked her why she never ran back home; she replied that she couldn't run away because her parents had been paid for her, so it would be unjust to her new owners to leave, as she was theirs. When it came to why she willingly allowed herself to be abused by paying customers, she again spoke of it as a case of justice. The first time a man came to use her, she managed to fight him off. She tried to do the same with the next man who came in, but he protested that she should not resist because he had paid her owner for the right to sex with her. Again, her sense of justice was such that she thought she would be acting wrongly not to give him what he had paid for.

"Which is justice, which is the thief?"

What is justice? Are there objective canons available to all? Is justice a universal metaphysical given? When Rowan Williams, Archbishop of Canterbury, suggested that aspects of Sharia law run parallel to British law, there was general uproar, as many felt the Muslim conception of civil justice differed radically from

9 *King Lear*, Act 4, Scene 6.

that of British law – to the point where their justice was another's injustice and vice versa.

In this book we are exploring the themes of justice and mercy from a biblical perspective. That's because the principles and practice of true justice align with the character and commands of God, as revealed in Scripture and pre-eminently personified in the life of Christ Jesus. Far from being a pragmatic plug-in, justice and mercy are at the heart of who God is, what God does, and how he wants to order his world.

1. Justice is God's DNA

In describing Jesus' ministry the apostle Matthew wrote: "I will put my Spirit upon him, and he will proclaim justice to the Gentiles" – that is, to the nations (Matthew 12:18). The Spirit of God on the Son of God manifests the justice of God. Justice is at the heart of God's being. Justice is a divine matter, a holy thing. Consequently to concern oneself with justice is to be led toward God; to concern oneself with God is to be led toward justice. Any consideration of justice cannot be done independent of the consideration, "Who is God?"

Because justice is a primary predicate of divinity, it would follow that the notion is franked like a watermark on every page of Scripture. It occurs in the Hebrew Old Testament as *tsedeq* over 200 times and in the Greek New Testament as *dikaiosyne* over 200 times. But it is the basis of all God says and does because he is just and righteous in all his ways. God's justice is disclosed in his very first statement to Adam and Eve as he reveals the divine order and the parameters of right and wrong: "You may surely eat of every tree of the garden, but of the tree of the knowledge of good and evil you shall not eat, for in the day that you eat of it you shall surely die" (Genesis 2:16–17).

When God formed a people for himself and revealed himself to them in the wilderness on Mount Sinai, his justice was revealed by coming as "law-giver". His redeemed people were to live before him in righteousness, in justice, by doing ("thou shalt") and by not doing ("thou shalt not").

Because justice is a primary divine attribute – and because we often in our sin and ignorance are far from God – this biblical notion of justice can seem alien to us, perhaps even "unfair". But the notion of justice is not a pragmatic construct plucked out of thin air and formulated to fashion society around. It is a design from God's decree. God is the judge of what is "just". God takes justice personally – and he also takes injustice very personally. Solomon the wise once wrote, "Whoever oppresses a poor man insults his Maker, but he who is generous to the needy honours him" (Proverbs 14:31). The prophet Micah told us that the mark of true religion – the kind of religion God receives – is "to do justice, and to love kindness, and to walk humbly with your God" (Micah 6:8).

Friedrich Nietzsche, perhaps the most influential philosopher of the twentieth century, understood that most systems of moral values are dependent on the idea of a God who is supreme Judge, one who underwrites our morals with rewards and punishments. Do away with God and you do away with ethics, and you can do what you want! Both Nietzsche (in *Thus Spake Zarasthustra*) and Fyodor Dostoyevsky (in *The Brothers Karamazov*) claimed that if God is dead, then everything is permissible – without a God to define right and wrong we can act as our fallen sinful nature desires. Ethics and justice for Nietzsche are merely pragmatically constructed rules for running society, without any divine sanction. Nietzsche's rejection of God led him to attribute society's inborn ethic as the evolved instinct of natural selection, the "survival of the fittest". According to this rule of the jungle – the rule of the gun – the most powerful impose their will on the weak.

Such an ideology was ripe for the picking with the rise of Nazism, leading to a "moral" justification of the gas chambers. It continues to influence post-modern nihilist and relativist thinking, whereby God is dismissed and right and wrong are determined by the free will of the one in power. Surely it is significant that atheistic nations, notably the former Soviet Union and Chinese communism, have been guilty of perhaps the worst systemic structural evil ever known. Here society was constructed without reference to a divine moral underpinning – and tens of millions were executed. Where there is no God everything is permissible.

Yet despite the best efforts of atheists to remove God and relativize right and wrong, humankind cannot so easily detach itself from God or God's DNA of justice. We are made in God's image, and we breathe by the very breath of God. There is an almost universal deep cry within the human soul for justice, and a deep protest when we see injustice, which even sin or self-interest cannot silence.

2. Justice is God's design plan

We have seen that Matthew recalls the prophecy of Isaiah concerning the Messiah that he will proclaim justice to the nations (Matthew 12:18). God seeks to order the nations according to his justice, and the mark of the divine Spirit upon Jesus is to herald that justice to the world. The prophet Isaiah declared God's intention to "make justice the line, and righteousness the plumb line" (Isaiah 28:17). As we have already noted, God's decrees for ordering society reflect his nature. The God of justice says we are to pursue "justice, and only justice" (Deuteronomy 16:20) and later declares: "Let justice roll down like waters" (Amos 5:24). Justice is not the pragmatic ordering of society that evolutionists would have us believe – a case of what works best for the fittest and strongest. Justice is not even so much about a judicial or legal code. It is essentially about right relationships with God. It is righteousness, right living with God and with neighbour and with nature. God and justice go hand in hand. Humankind made in God's image is thus to be marked by justice. When people in their free will reject justice, there is a tearing between them and God, between one and another.

Justice is life lived the way God ordained. The just God gives just laws to Israel at Sinai. These 613 rules for life are summed up by Jesus as: "Love God with all your heart, soul, mind and strength, and love your neighbour as yourself." Loving God and other people fulfils the law and fulfils justice.

Justice looks like love lived.

Injustice begins when we fail to love.

God's justice in Scripture looks like honest scales, no usury, no bribes, caring for creation, letting the land breathe every seven years, cancelling debts, not harvesting all but leaving the edge for the poor. Biblically, justice and mercy go hand in hand. Repeatedly four groups are singled out as special recipients of justice and mercy: *the poor, the alien, the widow, the orphan.* In other words, those who are most needy and most oppressed are to be the objects of justice, and God's anger is aroused where mercy is withheld.

I wonder what God thinks of a world that spends $31 billion on ice cream each year when $9 billion would install sanitation or water for the whole world. I wonder what God thinks of a world that spends $18 billion on facial cosmetics each year when $6 billion would give the whole world basic education.[10] I wonder what God thinks of a world which spends each year $2.4 trillion – that's 4.4 per cent of the global economy, according to the Global Peace Index – on "industries that create or manage violence", otherwise known as the defence industry, while economists have

---

10 http://www.givingwhatwecan.org/the-problem/it-can-be-solved.php

estimated that world poverty could be eradicated with one big push investment of $150 billion.[11]

3. Justice is God's delight

The one who proclaims justice to the nations is God's beloved, in whom his soul delights (Matthew 12:18). Those who proclaim and pursue justice among the nations, living in love with God and their neighbour, will find themselves beloved by God and delighted in by him. God says, "I the Lord love justice" (Isaiah 61:8), and so it is not surprising that this lover of justice loves the pursuer of justice. The command to pursue "only justice" is followed by the promise of divine blessing "that you may live and inherit the land" (Deuteronomy 16:20). Many traditions within the Christian family pursue an experience of the affections of God – the pietists, mystics, charismatics. But Scripture shows that the affections of God are directed toward the just and merciful. When we reach out to God and to our neighbour in justice and mercy, God reaches out to us in divine affirmation, attention and affection.

And the opposite is true. "The Lord saw it, and it displeased him that there was no justice … that there was no one to intercede" (Isaiah 59:15–16). Injustice, the failure to relate aright to God and neighbour, elicits God's indignation. The just God judges injustice. And so in Scripture *tsedeq* (justice) is often paired with *mishpat* (judgment) (see for example Isaiah 32:16). God's justice is not empty sentiment or emotion, and it is certainly not toothless. God expelled Israel from the land because of their failure to live justly. When David abused his power by taking Bathsheba and murdering Uriah God sent his prophet Nathan to expose the sin and pronounce punishment; and God's judgment was swift and fierce on the land. In Jesus' parable of the sheep and the goats

11 http://www.worldchanging.com/archives/001855.html

(Matthew 25) we are told that eternal destinies are determined by being able to demonstrate evidence of justice. God's just requirements, if not met, bring God's just punishment. But the just Judge is also merciful and, while we draw breath, he offers a way out of judgment on our sin, through Calvary's mercy.

4. Justice is God's double work

Jesus' mission was not concerned only with preaching and performing acts of justice; he was also the Suffering Servant who died to satisfy God's righteous judgment against our sin, and so to justify us.

The Old Testament term for justice *tsedeq* and its New Testament equivalent *dikaiosyne* may both also be translated as "righteousness". Justice and righteousness are in fact synonyms,[12] the first deriving from the Latin root and the second from the Old German. Justice and righteousness often carry different meanings in English, but are in fact synonymous in Scripture! The Bible calls for this righteousness that is justice in our relationships with both Creator and creation.

Righteousness is justice; justice is righteousness.

That said, the way in which the word is translated in the particular Bible we read will inadvertently determine how we apply that word. In modern usage "righteousness" can often be regarded as a religious or moral category, whereas "justice" may be seen as a legal or social category. But in Scripture both terms can convey the wide spectrum from moral uprightness, through covenantal relationship with God, to legal and judicial innocence. English versions of the Bible often translate the *dikaios* word group as "righteous" rather than "just", and this has at

---

12 See Bauer, Danker, Arndt, Gingrich on *dikaios*, pp. 195f; also Colin Brown (ed.), *New International Dictionary of New Testament Theology, Vol. 3*, pp. 352f. The semantic range of this Greek noun is "upright, just, righteous".

times skewed our theology, our mission and our discipleship. If in translation we choose "righteous" for *dikaios*, it may lead us to a very "religious" or so-called "spiritual" discipleship, whereas translating it as "just" takes us in a more "practical" or "social" direction. The Greek term embraces both senses without division.

There is an Italian proverb *"traduttore traditore"* – the translator is a traitor! We have often made a needless bifurcation between personal righteousness and social justice. Twentieth-century evangelicalism has tended to place the emphasis in interpreting *dikaios* on personal righteousness, the sinner's upright standing before a righteous God, through the imputation of Christ's righteousness by faith in Christ's substitutionary atonement.

A key text to support this would be: Romans 3:21–26 – a righteousness (*dikaiosyne*) for all who have faith in Jesus. In verse 25 Paul says that God presented Jesus as a propitiation to show his *dikaiosyne* "because in his divine forbearance he had passed over former sins".

Conversely, modern liberal theology and spirituality have tended toward interpreting *dikaios* as "just", directing the focus not so much to categories of personal sin and righteousness as to social justice. The confrontation with sin is understood not so much as an individual category but a corporate one, where structural social sin is challenged by the "just" ordering of relationships. For the liberal tradition, key themes would be drawn from such texts as Matthew 25:37 – the righteous or just (*dikaioi*) are those who have fed the hungry, given water to the thirsty, invited in the stranger, clothed the poor, and visited the sick or prisoner.

Some liberals despise the idea of a God punishing Jesus for our sins. Some evangelicals dismiss the idea of God caring profoundly about social justice. But both personal righteousness and social justice – the transformation of personal sin and structural sin – matter profoundly to God. Let's follow this admittedly slightly caricatured distinction between liberal and evangelical. The liberal tradition put more emphasis on the first three years of Jesus' mission and public ministry. Meanwhile evangelicals emphasize the last three days of Jesus' ministry – Good Friday to Easter Sunday, the cross and resurrection – where sin is dealt a death blow. The truth is, of course, that we must not bifurcate these two. We must be both a kingdom three-years and a Calvary three-days church. We preach righteousness through the cross for sinners and we preach the justice of the kingdom in society. There is no dichotomy between good news and good deeds – both are part of our church nature. Personal salvation and social transformation.

The evangelical statesman, John Stott, presented the biblical approach. In the 1980s he wrote his magisterial study on the atonement, *The Cross of Christ*, focusing on the salvation of the sinner through the substitutionary death of Christ. In the 1990s he wrote the prophetic book *Issues Facing Christians Today*, summoning the church to engage in transforming the ethical, political, creational, and social life of the world. I believe that one of the marks of what the Spirit of God has been doing in recent years is raising up a generation of integration: those passionate about both the gospel of salvation and social transformation; those committed to both personal justification and social justice.

5. Justice is God's goal for creation

The apostle Matthew quotes Isaiah in describing Jesus as the one whose ministry "brings justice to victory" (12:20).

Jesus' death and resurrection are the bringing of justice to victory – God's just judgment against sin and the demonic at

Calvary. The hope of Jesus' return and reign will finally and fully bring that justice to victory, when the living and the dead are brought before the just judgment seat of God. Jesus will bring justice to victory by establishing a new heaven on earth where justice or righteousness reigns, where a right relating to God and creation is in place. Justice will be brought to victory. Justice will have the last word. It is God's end game, the foundation of the eschatological vision of the new heaven and new earth.

The German philosopher Immanuel Kant identified deep within the human soul an innate sense of right and wrong, issuing in a desire for justice. For this universal awareness to have any meaning, he argued there must be some absolute law-giver, an arbiter of justice. He observed that justice is often not done in this world – in this life it would seem the unjust often prosper and the weak perish. Kant concluded that there must be a time and a place where justice is done, in the afterlife. In the epic movie *Gladiator* Russell Crowe plays a Roman general called Maximus, whose wife and son are murdered by the cruel emperor Commodus. Maximus promises that one day justice will be done: "I will have my revenge, in this life or the next." In fact God promises: "Vengeance is mine," and whether or not he exercises it in this life, he certainly will in the next. The unjust will not escape divine justice: the day is set, the terms are set, and justice will be done. Wrongs will be righted; the righteous will be rewarded.

Toward the end of Tolkien's classic book *The Lord of Rings* Sam Gamgee wakes from the deep sleep of an exhausted warrior, thinking everything is lost, only to quickly discover that all his friends are in fact with him. He cries out to the wizard he thought he had left for dead, "Gandalf! I thought you were dead! But then I thought I was dead! Is everything sad going to come untrue?"[13] Jesus will bring justice to victory. We have a heavenly

---

13 J. R. R. Tolkien, *The Return of the King*, p. 230.

vision, where justice reigns and injustices come undone, where the dead in Christ rise in glory, and the wicked rise to judgment. To that vision, and to that end, we must work.

Chapter 4

Leper-Lovers

The biggest disease today is not leprosy or
tuberculosis, but rather the feeling of being unwanted.
Mother Teresa

The late great rock 'n' roll legend Elvis wrote a classic song "The Wonder of You". There is a remarkably powerful line that speaks of becoming a king at the touch of a hand. One of the most radical, beautiful, extravagant things about Jesus was that the King of heaven touched untouchables and made them kings.

Jesus was a notorious, glorious leper-lover. The terms "leper" and "leprosy" come from the Greek verb *lepein* meaning to peel, to scale off. In Scripture leprosy is the generic term ascribed to any serious skin or muscle disease, not just the muscle-wasting illness we now call leprosy. Leviticus 13 defines a leper as someone who has contracted any sort of skin disease. In such an unfortunate case, the leprous person must leave their hair unkempt, cover their face, cry aloud, "Unclean, unclean!" and live alone until such time as the disease disappeared. This seemingly harsh isolation treatment was an attempt to localize the condition and keep it from contaminating others. One can only imagine the emotional trauma associated with such social exclusion, let alone the pain of the physical disfiguring.

Lepers suffered *physically*. The illness was one of discomfort if slight, or disfigurement if severe. There were no antibiotics or painkillers to ease the suffering.

Lepers suffered *socially*. They were excluded from entering any walled city, especially Jerusalem, and banished from their homes and communities. They were dislocated from normal social interaction and estranged from family and friends.

Lepers suffered *psychologically*. They were feared, blamed, shunned… imagine the mental anguish, the depression and despair, that they felt.

Lepers suffered *spiritually*. The illness was widely perceived as divine punishment for sin. But either way, sufferers were unable to attend worship in the Temple or the local assembly.

Who are the lepers today?

We might helpfully think of two categories: social lepers and spiritual lepers. The term "social lepers" is used in modern parlance to describe any person or people group who feels excluded, rejected, shunned, isolated, or demonized. We would include the poor, for sure, and the homeless, the ex-offender, the lad who left school at sixteen with nothing but bruises outside and in little hope of clawing his way off state handouts. Then there is the single mum or dad struggling to provide, to discipline, to cope. The have-nots always feel like lepers too – watching others live life while they seek to survive it. The elderly are often shut away in strange homes with strangers. Ex-cons are shunned. The mentally ill, the poor, immigrants, the homeless, the addicted… Socially the leper is anyone who is kept at arm's length, anyone from whom the rest disassociate themselves. It is anyone rejected for who they are and what they believe.

In South Africa under apartheid the Black community were made to feel like lepers before the Whites. But times change, and in Zimbabwe the white farmers today feel like the lepers. For some nations there was a time when those who were sexually promiscuous were scorned by the married and treated as pariahs. Perhaps today the pendulum has swung and, ironically, in a sexually permissive society, the young lady who decides to give the unique gift of her virginity to the man she will marry may experience derision and scorn, and thus made to feel a cultural leper. In a fashion-obsessed society, where we are told beauty is a super skinny size zero, the cuddly size fourteen can feel leprous. In a wartime community, the pacifist who cannot bear arms but chooses to work on the farm or down the mine, can feel leprous. In a strong religious community it may be the honest soul struggling with doubt. In an atheist community it may be the Christian; in a community of married couples it may be the single person or single parent or divorcee; in a fundamentalist church it is perhaps the theologically more liberal. In each case the leper is the one who doesn't fit in and is made to feel different.

Spiritually, we are all lepers: our sin has brought consequences. It has damaged us in every area – our bodies, relationships, minds, and destiny, as it separates us from God. We are all leprous in our souls until Christ touches them and makes them clean.

Journalist Malcolm Muggeridge went for a swim one morning in India. He saw a woman bathing naked and, though he was married, decided he would take her. As he swam nearer, his passion and lust raging, he lifted his eyes out of the water. Staring into the eyes of this frightened woman, he saw that she was a leper. His immediate thought was one of disgust at her. But then he realized it was he who was disgusting! Later he commented, "I suddenly recognized not how lecherous she was, but how leprous I was in my heart."[14] This was a key step on his way to finding Christ. Sadly, many remain unaware of their

---

14 Quoted on http://kelvinho-kh.blogspot.com/2009/06/jesus-christ-among-other-gods-1993.html

spiritual leprosy, giving rise to the need to preach the gospel and expose the sinful condition of the heart.

As we noted before, the evangelical tradition has generally focused its ministry on the sinner who can be cleansed by the forgiveness Jesus offers through the cross, whereas the more liberal tradition has tended to focus on the social leper, those rejected by the rest of society. Jesus loved both, Jesus touched and transformed both – leprosy outside and in. He is the leper-loving Lord.

The leper inclined to the Lord

Mark's Gospel tells us a leper came to Jesus, "imploring him, and kneeling said to him, 'If you will, you can make me clean'" (1:40).

According to rabbinical tradition, you could stone a leper if they came near you, in order to keep a safe distance and not become contaminated. But Jesus was no ordinary rabbi, and word got around the leper colonies that lepers could lean on Jesus. Why did this leper come to Jesus? He was desperate, and there was no one and nowhere else to go. He had heard the remarkable rumours that Jesus welcomed lepers. Not only that, he had heard that Jesus healed lepers. Lepers, whose lives are filled with rejection, are sensitively alert to those who will accept and those who will reject. Just one look at your eyes lets them know whether you are kind or cruel. We must ask ourselves: am I the sort of Christian – are we the sort of church – to which the lepers are drawn?

The Gospel account conveys real intensity in this man's approach; the Greek text uses three verbs of ongoing action: the leper kept *coming, kneeling, calling*. This man is desperate. He will break social convention, civil law, risk stoning and further pain if only to have the chance of a touch that will heal. Those who received from Jesus often had to be passionate and persistent. The woman with the haemorrhage had to push through the crowds; Zacchaeus the tax collector had to climb the tree; blind Bartimaeus had to shriek out loud for mercy; the woman with the dubious moral past had to gatecrash a party and let down her hair; the cripple had to be lowered through a roof on a bed by his friends. Like this leper, they were sick to death of their sickness; they believed Jesus could make a difference; they persisted in getting an audience with him; and they left transformed.

In his book *Crime and Punishment* Dostoyevsky shows that he has grasped that Christ welcomes lepers and that lepers look for Christ. Marmeladov is a broken, pitiful alcoholic, who has a wife, three small step-children, and an elder daughter by his first wife. They all live a bleak poverty-ridden existence because of Marmeladov's alcoholism. Under duress his eldest daughter Sonia has become a prostitute to support her family. When the tavern owner challenges Marmeladov's right to be pitied for his plight, Marmeladov shows he has a revelation of the leper-loving Christ:

> *The one who will take pity on me is him that hath pity*
> *for all men ... he is our judge. He will come this day, and*
> *inquire: "And where is the daughter that hath not spared*
> *herself for the sake of her harsh-tongued and consumptive*
> *stepmother and for young children that are not her own*
> *kith and kin? Where is the daughter who took pity on her*
> *earthly father, an obscene drunkard, undismayed by his*
> *bestial nature?" And he will say unto her, "Come unto me!*
> *I have already forgiven thee once" ... he will raise up his*
> *voice to us, saying unto us: "Come out, ye drunkards, come*
> *out, O ye that are weak, come out, ye that live in shame!"*
> *And we shall come out, and shall not be ashamed, and shall*
> *stand before him. ... And the wise and the learned will*
> *raise up their voices, saying: "Lord! Why dost thou receive*

them?" And he will say unto them: "Because they none
of them ever believed themselves worthy of it..." And he
will stretch out his hand to us, and we shall fall down, and
weep...and understand everything.[15]

The Lord inclined to the leper

"Filled with compassion, Jesus reached out his hand and
touched the man. 'I am willing,' he said. 'Be clean!' Immediately
the leprosy left him and he was cured" (Mark 1:41–42 NIV).
The Greek word translated compassion is *splagchnizomai,* the
root meaning of which refers to the bowels, the inner depths
of a person. We would say that Jesus was "gutted" when he
saw this man. The crowd may have been appalled at a leper in
public; Jesus was stirred deep within by tenderness. I have often
reflected on the contrast between the Judeo-Christian God and
the Greco-Romans gods. The latter are indifferent, unmoved,
dispassionate, unimpressed by mere mortals. The word *apatheia*
was coined to describe them – apathetic, indifferent to us. But
the Christian God is a "pathetic" God, filled with pathos, moved
by us; he feels for us. The celebrated atheist Richard Dawkins
famously described our universe as "nothing but blind pitiless
indifference" claiming that "DNA neither cares nor knows".[16]
But Jesus shows this to be a lie when he reveals there is a Heart
at the heart of the universe.

The oldest attested text of Mark actually uses a different
word from "compassion" here in verse 41, employing the term
orgisthein. This word, from which we get our term orgy, conveyed
the sense of violent emotion, anger, burning passion. Jesus' love
was not "sentimental" – he was angered, incensed, pained, and
protesting at the ravages of sin that had destroyed this man's

---

15 Fyodor Dostoyevsky, *Crime and Punishment*, pp. 29–30.
16 Dawkins, *River out of Eden*, p. 155.

life. He was angry at the leprosy, not the leper, and his anger led to action. The leper would not be leprous for long. Mark tells us that the very first thing Jesus did was to stretch toward and touch. The leper stood a little removed from Jesus. Jesus moved toward him, leaning, stretching, and touched the leper. Everyone else encountering a leper took a step backwards – Jesus stepped forwards. Jesus could merely have spoken the word and banished the leper's condition, but that tender touch meant as much to the leper as the physical healing.

Jesus Christ is no absent divine waving at the world from a distance.

Jesus is there, with the people, with the suffering lepers, stretched toward them, touching and healing them. The National Lottery's tagline is "You've got to be in it to win it." So it is with the world: you've got to be in it to win it, you've got to touch it to transform it and see the kingdom of God break through.

Jesus stretched toward lepers. Sadly the church often pulls away. Medieval church walls had built in "squint holes", narrow slits, so that lepers could watch the services from outside without entering and contaminating those inside. What a sad stain such architecture is on the soul of the church. Why did the world take Princess Diana into their hearts, probably more than other royals? Because of that unforgettable image of her tenderness as she held AIDS orphans and embraced landmine victims. She extended her hands to the suffering when others kept a discreet distance, waving gloved hands from Bentleys.

The leper was instantly healed, and his healing was more than skin deep.

His whole life was transformed: he was free of disease, the barriers that separated him from others now removed. He was at peace with himself, whole inside and out. Jesus welcomed lepers with skin disease and lepers with soul disease: he touched and transformed both. The world is full of lepers: socially diseased, needy, broken, rejected, spiritually lost, dead in sin. Like Jesus we are to be leper-lovers. We the church are to be a leper colony. Stretching toward them, letting them know they can incline toward us.

Chapter 5

Remember the Poor, Remember the Lord

While you are poor and he is king you shall not be forgot.[17]
William Cowper

Many years ago, when I was training for the priesthood at theological college, a game was set for us in pastoral theology. The class was divided into two groups. One group was taken outside and not told the rules or purpose of the game, the other group inside the classroom were told the rules. Each person was given ten Snap playing cards, and the aim was to get five matching pairs.

The group outside were brought back into the room, whereupon the other group pounced on them, trying to swap with them to get matching pairs. All this without talking. As a member of the enlightened group I immediately saw the way to win. By standing at the door as the others came in, I was the first, using sign language, to get them to show me their cards, and to get them to swap for a matching pair that I wanted. I was not bothered about helping them get their own matching pairs, because the aim was to win... surely? Soon I had a full set of five pairs and sat down, the winner. I watched as others scrambled to get matched pairs. Those not privy to the rules remained largely

---

17 From the poem "For the Poor".

bemused, with just a few cottoning on and becoming more canny in their swapping.

At the end the convener pointed out that we in the room knowing the rules had the advantage and the ability to prosper. The pastoral theology tutor pointed out that we had had a choice whether we used our power of knowledge for self-interest or to help others. Some in the class were commended for seeking to assist those not privy to the rules. I was highlighted as both the shrewd clear winner and the abuser of power and people. My delight in victory was quickly snatched away.

Are we in it to win it, or are we here to help?

The text we are considering in this chapter is often missed and seldom taught. Yet Leviticus 19:9–10 highlights the heart of God and his instruction to his people on how to live – not grabbing all the gain we can, but living with eyes and hands open to others.

Remember the poor

"You shall not reap your field right up to its edge, neither shall you gather the gleanings after your harvest … neither shall you gather the fallen grapes of your vineyard. You shall leave them for the poor…" (Leviticus 19:9–10).

God decreed that provision be made for the less privileged, the non-landowners, the pilgrims and the poor, to gather gleanings from the harvest. We actually see this enacted in Ruth 2, where Ruth was gleaning behind the reapers and Boaz instructs the workers in his field to allow her to take what remains. And leaving pickings for the poor was never merely optional. There is no appeal to the conscience, or to the compassionate concern of the harvester – it is a straightforward command: harvesters must leave part of the harvest for the poor. In God's eyes it actually belongs to them – the land may be the farmer's, but God who made the crop grow owns the crop and gives instructions on how it is to be used. This verse is not about charity or benevolence; it is about the gleaning rights God gives to the poor.

Now, most of us are not farmers and so this text cannot be applied directly. But we cannot escape its pointed finger so easily. Most of us have an income, and I believe this text calls for part of that income to be left untouched, unharvested, specifically left aside and from which the poor are to directly benefit. It is true that taxpayers already contribute indirectly to the poor, but so did the farmers of Bible times through their temple tithes and taxes. The farmer was also instructed to make a direct provision for the poor, and so ought we. Over and above your church tithe, why not give to support a charity that works for the poor, or pay extra on groceries that are fair trade, or set aside a little extra to support orphans in their education and provision? At the very least you can pay £10 and buy Peter Grant's outstanding book *Poor No More* and find creative ways of looking to the poor.

In 2010 the average UK salary for a man was about £30,000, the average for a woman £24,000. (The discrepancy begs the question about equity…) The average salary in the UK for a chief executive was around £100,000.[18] Compare that to the average Ethiopian salary of £90 per annum. How do we imagine half the world actually survives on less than £1.30 a day? Many don't. There are 30,000 people who die every day because of poverty. The number of children who will die today from diarrhoea because of dirty water or no sanitation is 4,000. In the time it takes you to read this chapter, 600 people will have breathed their last because they are too poor to live.

These are not mere numbers but people intricately made in the image of God. They are made for God, known to God by

---

18 http://www.thisismoney.co.uk/money/article-1709280/Best-paid-jobs-A-guide-UK-salaries.html

name, died for in person at Calvary, whose every hair on their heads has been counted by God.

Meanwhile, the world spends $18 billion a year on facial cosmetics and $15 billion on perfumes; $11 billion is spent on ice cream in Europe and $20 billion in the USA; $17 billion is spent on pet food in USA and Europe together. Every billion spent on cosmetics or pet food could save one million lives.

Jesus once said, "The poor you will always have with you," and it's probably the case that we won't ever make poverty history. But we could try! At the very least we could share a bit of our harvest with the poor!

I have a friend called Martin. An ex-career paratrooper turned military market stall trader, he's not a Christian but he likes Jesus. Martin often says to me, "Jesus was airborne." He is claiming Jesus as one of his people. He asked me once: "Is your guv'nor a socialist?" I said no. If Jesus was a socialist he would want farms to be state-owned or owned by a collective with an equal share in the harvest. But God does not say, "Sell the farm and share it evenly among the poor." Nor does he say, "Divide up the farm and give everyone equal portions." But he does say, "Harvest it and leave some for the poor." We are not called to be like St Francis, selling everything we have and living poor, dependent on God and charity. We are called to work with all our might, and be good stewards of what we've been given, investing it, making money and sharing with the poor.

There are many causes of poverty, but most come down to an accident of birth. The poor chose the wrong parents. Laziness, wantonness, illness, being sinned against, usury, oppression, national disaster, lack of education, wars... all of these play their part. But God doesn't say that only those who have a "legitimate" reason to be poor can expect assistance. We are to consider the poor, not categorize the poor.

The early church cared for the poor. In Jerusalem we see they fed the hungry. In Acts11:28–30 they made collections for the needy victims of famine. When Paul was tested about his faith by the Jerusalem elders, he was told to "remember the poor" (Galatians 2:10). The early church cared for the poor; parts of the modern church seem just to want to get rich. Prosperity preachers baptize greed and so preach a false gospel. "God wants you rich!" Wrong! God never said, "Grow bigger harvests." He did say, "Share with the poor." And to those who do, God will often grant a bumper harvest. The spirit of the world makes us greedy; the Spirit of God makes us care for the needy. The devil tempts with this: "All these I will give you, if you will fall down and worship me" (Matthew 4:9), whereas Jesus offers salvation by testing with this: "Go, sell all that you have and give to the poor … and come, follow me" (Mark 10:21).

A senior businessman once told me how, at a board meeting, accountants' analysts suggested he could get certain things manufactured much more cheaply, with more profit their end, if the goods were manufactured in China rather than their existing factories in India. My friend protested, "I'd rather the workers had a better deal, than our business had a cheaper product and a bigger profit." He understood those biblical principles "remember the poor" and "don't reap to the edge of the field". He didn't stay long at that company.

The harvester is not to contemplate and compare his harvest with another farmer who has a greater harvest, but to consider someone who has no harvest. Sadly, rather than compare what we have with those who have less, we usually compare what we have with those who have more. This leads us away from being grateful with what we have and generous to those with less, toward being dissatisfied, or jealous, and striving for more.

I recall one day being jealous when I compared my cruddy second-hand car to the two new cars my friend had recently bought (one for him, one for his wife). That day I met a poor man whose shoe soles were falling off. The very same day I had also been jealous when someone had told me of their second home, a ski chalet in the Alps, when I lived in a rented, draughty, damp old vicarage. But then the man with the holes in his shoes told me that his tent had been stolen and all the thieves had left him were four pegs!

Sometimes we feel sorry for ourselves when we should thank God for what we have. We need to open our eyes and dig deeper in our pockets for those who have next to nothing. Biblically we aren't to compare and contrast with those who have more, but think of those with less and share. The old mealtime grace said: "For what we are about to receive may the Lord make us truly thankful and ever mindful of the needs of others." Generally we are neither truly thankful nor ever mindful of the needs of others. Considering our "harvest", and the fact that many have no harvest, ought to make us both truly thankful and ever mindful.

Remember the Lord

"I am the Lord your God" (Leviticus 19:10).

By remembering the poor we will remember the Lord. By remembering the Lord we will remember the poor. Songwriter and church planter David Ruis devotes much of his ministry and most of his money to the poor. On his arm is a tattoo: "Consider the poor". On one occasion he was in Starbucks buying a coffee when a woman saw his tattoo and screamed demonically, "Why should I?", proceeding to let rip a whole load of bile against the poor and how it was their fault, and she was not responsible, and he shouldn't dump a guilt trip on her.

Remember the poor? Why should I? Because God is God and God says so! Following his imperative comes God's indicative. The imperative to leave something for the poor is wed to the indicative – because God is the Lord! God doesn't make an appeal to the heart but to the will. Emotions are fickle, moved today by the poor, moved tomorrow by the seagulls. Feelings fluctuate but commands stand. God cannot rely on our feelings to do the right thing so he must dictate to our wills. This command comes from God, not from the altruistic ideas of a man called Moses. The land and crops and good harvests are all gifts from God. This is direct divine decree that leaves no room for debate. And only a fool would want to ignore what matters to God. If compassion will not motivate you to help the poor, then try obedience.

We remember the poor because God remembers the poor

To consider God is to consider what he considers. The poor are never far from his thoughts. The first thing stated in the manifesto of Jesus was: "to preach good news to the poor". The lost, the last and the least in this world's thinking are generally first in God's mind, and so should be in our ministry. We remember the poor because God takes it as a personal affront if we don't. We remember the poor because God remembers if we do and if we don't. Come judgment day, you don't ever want to hear Jesus say, "As you did not do it to one of the least of these, you did not do it to me" (Matthew 25:45).

- God sees fat Dives stuffing his face while Lazarus sits at his gate starving
- God sees the children unable to sleep because of aching empty stomachs
- God sees a mother weeping, knowing tomorrow won't be any easier
- God sees the desperate father turn to drink, drowning his pain and shame

- God sees the pubescent girl prostituted for the price of a bowl of rice

- God sees all this and is pained, he has compassion, and he wants us to help.

In Acts 10 we are introduced to Cornelius, a Roman centurion who receives first an angelic visitation, then a personal visit from the apostle Peter, and finally a visit from the Holy Spirit. Without even asking for it. What has this man done to merit a visit from angels, from apostles, and from the Spirit of God? Because God was watching him, and God was impressed by him, and God wanted to bless him! The angel explains: "Your gifts to the poor have come up as a memorial offering to God." Now this is a real charismatic theology: visitations by angels, visions to apostles, baptisms in Spirit, speaking in tongues – all precipitated when one man got God's attention by giving to the poor.

Elsewhere God tells us the pros and cons in remembering the poor. The wisdom of God is to be generous. Only the fool ignores the poor.

Pro: "Whoever is generous to the poor lends to the Lord, and he will repay him for his deed" (Proverbs 19:17).

Con: "Whoever closes his ear to the cry of the poor will himself call out and not be answered" (Proverbs 21:13).

Pro: "Whoever has a bountiful eye will be blessed, for he shares his bread with the poor" (Proverbs 22:9)

Con: "Whoever oppresses a poor man insults his Maker" (Proverbs 14:31a)

Pro: "he who is generous to the needy honours [God]" (Proverbs 14:31b)

Con: "Do not rob the poor… for the Lord will plead their cause and rob of life those who rob them" (Proverbs 22:22–23).

We need a generation of godly economists, traders, and fund managers who can create wealth *ethically*, then invest it for a return in changed lives.

At the very least the whole financial crisis and credit crunch in recent years must cause us to ask questions about wealth creation – about greed and the value we place on money. Maybe God has been shaking the finance world because it reaped a harvest to its edges. In a time of global recession, credit crunch and economic turndown, we need to remember the poor, and remember the Lord. When almost everyone is tightening their belts, yet a handful of bankers in the City can receive a share of a £6.8 billion bonus payout, we must ask, did they reap the harvest to the edge of the field? Was anything left for the poor? When in late 2008 the American economy found itself facing serious problems, and the US Senate proposed a rescue plan of $700 billion to stabilize the economy, we must ask why she is in such financial trouble. How is it that $700 billion can be found, when they couldn't find a mere $5 billion to save six million lives?[19]

Consider the poor

How then should we respond? We must identify the poor and then identify with the poor. We must stand with and for the poor. We must, as a church, cultivate and convey God's heart for the poor. We must give to the poor. We must preach the good news to the poor. Whether it's lobbying your MP, informing local media, buying ethically, shunning wastefulness, giving generously, acting hospitably, or volunteering for local action, there is no

19 http://www.givewell.org/files/Cause1-2/+UNICEF/Lancet%20can_
the_world_affort_child_surv.pdf

shortage of ways to live more mercifully and justly. We are spoilt for choice – let's not be too spoilt to choose.

I close this chapter with the words sometimes used by the US Evangelical Lutheran Church at the end of its liturgy: "Go in peace – remember the poor."

Chapter 6

Crisis and the Cry "Justice"

Justice and power must be brought together, so that whatever is just may be powerful, and whatever is powerful may be just.
Blaise Pascal

We have already reflected on God's heart for justice and our need to lend a hand for justice. The theme of this chapter is the need for us to intercede for justice. Jesus instructed us to pray daily, "Our Father in heaven, hallowed be your name; your kingdom come; your will be done on earth as in heaven." The first subject for prayer is not ourselves, not for our needs to be met, our battles to be won, or our issues resolved... but for God's name to be honoured and held in awe. The second petition contributes to fulfilling the first: God's name is honoured as his righteousness is enacted and his divine justice is manifested. Praying for justice and righteousness, praying against injustice and unrighteousness, is not an abstraction but a concrete action. It is not one of the least but one of the most practical things we can do for justice. When we pray for God's will to be done on earth as in heaven we pray that the will of the Just One will be done here. The prayer is for heaven to come to earth. In heaven there is no poverty, no oppression, no racism, no sexism, no intellectualism, no ageism, no fear, no abuse, no hunger, no slavery, no crime, no victims, no tears. This paradise paradigm is to be applied against our world, and we must pray as well as work to see earth aligned with heaven.

There is of course more often than not a great gulf between heaven's justice and the world's unrighteousness. And that's why Jesus taught the following parable, so that we should always pray and not lose heart (Luke 18:1).

We see the crisis of justice in the land (Luke 18:1–8)

"There was a judge who neither feared God nor respected man. And there was a widow in that city who kept coming to him and saying, 'Give me justice against my adversary.'" Luke 18:2–3

The picture Jesus paints was one that was all too common in first-century Israel. Jewish law had previously made provision for appeal courts, where there were three judges – one chosen by the plaintiff, one chosen by the defendant, and one who was independent. However, this threefold chord that was meant to guarantee a fair hearing was abolished in the first century AD by Herod and the Romans. They established a new judicial process in which a single magistrate heard the case. The system soon became notorious for the potential to bribe the magistrate. There was a Roman saying of magistrates in the empire: "They pervert justice for a plate of meat." In the Hebrew tongue these magistrates were called *dayyaneh gezerot*, meaning "prohibition judge", but they were so corrupt that they gained the similar sounding but sharp nickname *dayyaneh gezelot* which meant "thieving judge".

Jesus presents to us a widow. In the ancient world, with no husband to provide and protect her and no state pension to live on, she relied on the mercy of others. This widow is oppressed by an adversary and seeks recompense from a judge who, it turns out, feared neither God nor anyone else.

We might well ask why she stood alone, powerless and harassed before this unjust judge. Why was no one beside her, defending her cause? The Old Testament Law and Prophets often highlighted widows and the poor as requiring special care in the land, such that care for the widow and the poor became a criterion for whether God would bless or severely judge the nation. God spoke to Israel through Isaiah: "Cease to do evil, learn to do good; seek justice, correct oppression; bring justice to the fatherless, plead the widow's cause" (Isaiah 1:16–17). What a sadly familiar picture Jesus paints: a judge with no fear of God, no respect for people, and a widow facing an oppressive adversary.

No fear of God

The name of God is blasphemed, mocked, and used as a swear word. Elderly street preachers are mobbed, then arrested for breach of the peace. Employees are forbidden to wear crosses at work. Church buildings are emptied of worshippers and turned into libraries, restaurants, carpet warehouses, flats, and now mosques. In the last 100 years church attendance in the UK has been consistently in decline. The Church of England has seen a 50 per cent drop in membership; Methodism a 70 per cent drop; Baptists 50 per cent; the United Reformed Church 75 per cent.[20] These figures are even more severe when we consider that the population has increased by 80 per cent from 37 million to 62 million over that time. In most denominations in the UK the church is haemorrhaging. Sin advances while the fear of God is almost non-existent.

---

20 http://www.whychurch.org.uk/trends.php

No respect for people

There is a natural law that, where the fear of God is lost, the respect of man is lost. Honouring the Creator God causes us to honour people and the place he has made. Yet lawlessness fills our streets with feral gangs, drug dealing, and knife crimes. There were 10,912,000 crimes reported in England and Wales alone between 2005 and 2006.[21] Britain's prisons are at breaking point; by June 2011, the prison population in England and Wales had grown to 84,635, having been recorded at around 44,628 between 1992 and 1993.[22] In the year 2007, 8,196 pregnancies were reported of girls under sixteen, of which 50 per cent ended in abortions (having risen from 40 per cent in 1996).[23] Between 1996 and 2005 there was a 2054 per cent increase in syphilis.[24] Top bankers paid themselves billions in bonuses while unemployment rose, the poor had their homes foreclosed, and the gap between rich and poor grew ever wider. No fear of God, no respect for people, the widow oppressed by adversaries… it is as Gandalf said: "The darkness is deepening."

In Mark 9 we see the disciples are trying to drive out a demon from a boy but are unable to do so. Jesus, however, instantly comes along and exorcizes the demon. The disciples ask why they could not remove the demon, and Jesus replies, "This kind cannot be driven out by anything but prayer" (Mark 9:29, where some New Testament manuscripts add "and fasting"). Martyn Lloyd-Jones in his classic work *Revival* said that we need revival when the demon is in too deep. When our best efforts, like the disciples, cannot exorcize society's evil, then we need Jesus to

21 http://www.crimestoppers-uk.org/crime-prevention/latest-crime-statistics
22 http://www.prisonreformtrust.org.uk/Portals/0/Documents/Fact%20File%20June%202011%20web.pdf
23 http://www.telegraph.co.uk/health/healthnews/4839713/Teenage-abortions-hit-record-as-under-16-pregnancy-rate-soars.html
24 http://www.avert.org/std-statistics-uk.htm

come in his power. Nothing but a personal visitation of Christ and a power encounter of his Spirit will put things right. I believe we live in an age when the demon is in too deep. I know that most of our politicians and police are doing their very best, but they are overwhelmed by the task. I no longer have confidence that they can put things right. Do you?

The need for revival

Our only hope is heaven-sent revival – Christ visiting and exorcising evil. Jonathan Edwards, the great eighteenth-century American leader, experienced a remarkable revival in New England. God descended suddenly as Edwards preached a now famous sermon entitled "Sinners in the hands of an angry God".[25] Protestants make pilgrimage to the Yale Library where Edwards' personal books and writings are kept, and they wax lyrical about actually holding the manuscript of the sermon. It is almost as if they believe it is magical in its power to precipitate revival, as it did the Great Awakening in 1734 which lasted for sixteen years. But what is less well known is that Edwards had preached that very sermon before, to no effect. Clearly the power was not in the text as such.

In fact the fire only fell on America when Edwards preached this sermon after he had prayed and fasted for two days, not sleeping a wink but beseeching God to come. When the time came Edwards read the sermon in his customary dull fashion, for he was no orator. He held a candle close, as his eyes were not strong. But as he spoke, God thundered – and the Spirit fell. People were convicted and cried aloud for mercy from God. For sixteen years many were brought to Christ and the moral fabric of society was transformed. Edwards wrote:

---

25 http://www.ccel.org/ccel/edwards/sermons.sinners.html

If we are not to expect that the devil should go out of a particular person, under a bodily possession, without extraordinary prayer, or prayer and fasting, how much less should we expect to have him cast out of the land, and the world, without it?[26]

We see the cries for justice from the widow

"Because this woman keeps bothering me, I will give her justice" (Luke 18:5).

"And the Lord said: 'Hear what the unrighteous judge says. And will not God give justice to his elect, who cry to him day and night?'" (Luke 18:6–7).

The widow wasn't willing to lie down and die. She did not give up or let up. Her cause was just and so she gave the judge no rest. She gave herself no rest. The uncaring, unjust judge finally gave in to the constant attrition of petition by widow.

Of course the church must persist in standing for and stating the case of justice – speaking, lobbying, writing, petitioning, voting – making justice the constant cry of the church. But that's not how Christ applies the story. If the unjust judge grants justice to the wearying widow, says Jesus, how much more will the caring King of heaven, our heavenly Father, respond tenderly to the persistent tear-soaked prayers of his saints? Jesus says this parable is a metaphor; this woman is a model for us – to press and pursue a God who does care, so that justice might be done. Jesus promises that, just as the judge granted justice to the persistent widow, so will our gracious God, our heavenly Father. "And will not God give justice to his elect, who cry to him day and night? … I tell you, he will give justice to them speedily" (Luke 18:7–8).

---

26 http://www.ccel.org/e/edwards/works1.ix.vi.iii.html

Our prayers must be passionate

The widow "cried out". The original Greek term is an intense word that means "to break forth in shouts, cry aloud in anguish". It was used of the shrieks of demons exiting!

Faced with a tidal wave of injustice, this is not a time for passionless, soulless, half-hearted, half-baked, polite, muttering prayers!

Our prayers must be persistent

The widow cried out "day and night". Isaiah spoke of taking no rest and giving God no rest "until he establishes Jerusalem" (Isaiah 62:6–7). We must pray and not cease for God to establish Zion in our churches, businesses, communities, streets, schools, and homes.

Scripture commends the widow Anna, a prophetess, for awaiting the redemption of Jerusalem. She worshipped and prayed "day and night" at the temple and so got to see the Christ child and to know God's redemption had arrived. God has ordained that passionate, persistent prayer brings breakthrough. God will bring justice for his chosen ones who cry out to him day and night.

We need to passionately persist in prayer for two reasons: it proves and it removes.

Persistent prayer *proves* our sincerity and our seriousness. It shows God we mean business. This is not a whim, a mere fancy; we don't treat God as a fairy godmother waving a wand to meet our wish.

Secondly, persistent prayer *removes*. It is the prayer of attrition that removes the obstacles of the world, the flesh, and the devil. In Daniel 10 we read that Daniel sought God and humbled himself for his nation. Eventually an angel appears who says that he was despatched with an answer twenty-one days earlier, but was challenged by the demonic prince of Persia and had to summon the archangel Michael to help. Daniel's prayers for twenty-one days brought breakthrough. The devil is the father of injustice and unrighteousness. Prayer is warfare against him. Prayer for justice and righteousness may always be contested, but we must push through in protest and prayer.

George Müller, the nineteenth-century founder of orphanages and schools, lived a life of warring prayer. He vowed to pray daily for the conversion of five friends. One came to faith within months; two came to Christ ten years later, and the fourth came to Christ after twenty-five years. The fifth became a Christian at George's funeral!

South African apartheid took forty-six years of prayer and protest to be dismantled. American slavery took 257 years of prayer and protest to be outlawed. Clearly we need to gain God's heart and spirit of intercession against injustice if we are going to make serious headway. We need to pray informed prayers, Bible in one hand, newspaper in the other. And of course there are many websites that will fuel our prayers with up-to-date information.

When the demon is in too deep for the disciples to remove, we need the Holy Spirit to come in revival power to establish God's just kingdom. Every revival begins with passionate, persistent, breakthrough prayer. Often it is no more than a handful of people who see the crisis and get crying. In the eighteenth century England had no fear of God and no respect for men. Deism, the doctrine of a God who has walked away from the world's stage, dominated the churches: God was not there and God didn't care. Immorality filled the streets – the 160 crimes punishable by death did little to stem crime, as crowds watched daily hangings for pleasure. Every sixth house was a gin house; prostitution and all manner of sexual perversion were rife. Britain was on the brink of civil war just like her neighbour France. The demon was in real deep.

But God stirred a handful of students in Oxford to found the "Holy Club", among them John Wesley (with his brother Charles) and George Whitefield. They eagerly sought God and did good deeds for the poor and the prisoners. They consecrated themselves to holiness, to alms-giving and to being Spirit-filled. They took hold of God and finally God met them one by one – John Wesley at a Moravian meeting in London, George Whitefield following several months of prayer. Like Jacob of old they took hold of God and would not let him go until he blessed them. And he did. Through them God took hold of the nation, sparking the Evangelical Awakening and the Great Awakening in America. The spiritual climate changed, the social and moral tone was transformed, as God's justice and his kind, kingly rule came. In the end, when France had a civil war, Britain had a revival.

Will you pray?

When I first began writing this chapter I felt the Lord speak clearly to my soul: "How much worse does it have to get before my chosen ones start crying out day and night for justice?" As I returned to it, I had just witnessed a drug addict pushing through a crowd, having stolen a woman's purse to fuel his crazed addiction; I observed a drug deal in broad daylight; I picked my way through the puddles of blood painting the pavement from the previous night's violent assaults. I then walked past a pub where my ten-year-old son remarked that a man had been killed just there, stabbed to death for a wrong look.

I live in Oxford. Among its noble ancient college and cathedral spires is all manner of evil. What should I do? What could I do? The police have no time for petty crime – their hands are full trying to find the serial sex attacker who has struck here for the fifth time in a week. God again spoke to me: "Prayer is not the least thing you can do, but the best." And so I have resolved to intensify my prayers for justice – for the drug dealer to be saved, for the empty youths to find satisfaction in God not skunk, for the streets to be washed by tears of repentance, for the sex offender to be arrested, for righteousness and justice to be established.

Jesus says: "And will not God give justice to his elect, who cry to him day and night? … I tell you, he will give justice to them speedily. Nevertheless, when the Son of Man comes, will he find faith on earth?" (Luke 18:7–8). Jesus is looking for and returning for a believing, interceding, breakthrough church. Praying for, preaching, petitioning for, promoting and practising God's justice. If he came now, would he find that in us? Or would he find a hibernating church that has given up on prayer and given in to church decline and the rise of unrighteousness and injustice?

Do you want to be part of the best answer?

On your walls, O Jerusalem, I have set watchmen;
all the day and all the night they shall never be silent.
You who put the Lord in remembrance,
take no rest, and give him no rest
until he establishes Jerusalem and makes it a praise in
the earth.
Isaiah 62:6–7

Chapter 7

The Robbery of Bribery

Every man has his price.
Idiom

We all have a tendency to steer our way through some form of bribery. On becoming a parent I quickly realized just how often bribery functions as an alternative tool for discipline. Chocolate keeps infants quiet; warnings of withholding pocket money or presents stop children from whining, or get them to tidy their messy bedrooms. Promises of rewards for success in exams, or even gifts given for good school reports, all format a psychology of bribery in the child.

Growing up, I learned quickly that religion and bribery could go hand in hand. My mother would ply us with fruit gums to keep us silent in church, such that ever since then in sermons I salivate, programmed like Pavlov's dogs, awaiting my fruit gum. Of course, my dear mum wouldn't conceive of it as a bribe – more of a medication, or even a reward.

There is of course the concept of reward within the nature of Christianity, as well as its opposite, punishment. God is the rewarder of those who earnestly seek him (Hebrews 11:6); prayer, study, obedience, service, bring reward; whereas disobedience, and coldness of heart toward God and his world, closes God's hand. Again, investment of the talents God gives brings divine reward, whereas misuse of that which God gives brings divine displeasure (Matthew 25:26–30). But clearly it would be wrong to see this as inculcating a value structure in which we are bribed to be righteous, or where God is bribed to bless. No, God is neither bribed nor bribing; what he offers is blessing and reward for doing the right thing.

A bribe is gaining something by doing the wrong thing or not doing the right thing. Bribery and its ugly sister "kickback" may be defined as "the giving or receiving of any 'valuable item' (cash or kind) in order to influence an official act or a business decision". The bribes that are offered are generally material – money, gifts – but they can be almost anything offered – loyalty, silence, sexual favours, promotion… whatever entices or buys an individual to act against what is right.

The world's economy is, and always has been, based on the exchange of goods and services for money. This exchange can be right and proper, but it turns from the legitimate to the immoral bribe when the exchange involves the illicit or morally questionable – either to cover up truth, disadvantage a third party, gain something illegal, or persuade an official to act impartially. And so on. Essentially a bribe is a gift which causes the recipient to act favourably and with bias toward the giver. There is often a third party involved who loses out. They may lose justice or a contract, or something that is theirs by right, to the briber.

Many see the bribe as just another currency in economic transaction. Indeed in some less economically developed countries bribery is a normative form of currency that everyone understands. However, in its worst form the bribe leads to direct injury and injustice, as a blind eye is turned to the rightful claim of an innocent, and the truth is silenced. Generally those who suffer are the poorest and least powerful, for they have nothing to use for leverage. So often we use the term "bribery and corruption", for in truth there are no honest bribes.

1. God ordains a society where bribes are banned

Throughout the Old Testament – Law, Prophets and Wisdom books – God repeatedly speaks against bribery. For God bribery is a heinous sin; indeed it seems to be classed among the worst sins. The prophet Amos thunders (5:12): "I know how many are your transgressions and how great are your sins – you who afflict the righteous, who take a bribe, and turn aside the needy in the gate" (that is, deprive the poor of justice in the courts). God regards the bribe as a tool of oppression and deprivation. God told Moses to appoint judges in all the towns in Israel who were to judge with "righteous judgment", not perverting justice by showing partiality; they will "not accept a bribe, for a bribe blinds the eyes of the wise and subverts the cause of the righteous" (Deuteronomy 16:18–19).

God is aware that fallen sinful men will squabble, fall out, and do wrong by each other. He takes seriously the human propensity for wickedness in society, and seeks to control it by appointing judges who stand in the place of God, making his judgment and establishing his justice. There were to be judges "in every tribe and in every town", not just in the big cities, so that everyone might have access to justice. The Hebrew text states that there should be a judge "at every gate" – not behind secret doors, not in an imposing intimidating building, but in a public place of transaction where the judge could sit and hear cases, and where everyone could have access and where crowds could gather and witness.

The judges are warned: "You shall not pervert justice" (Deuteronomy 16:19). The role of a judge is not to make up law but to administer it. There is benchmark, a standard set by the righteous/just nature and character of God, revealed in his laws and decrees. Judges are warned not to "show favouritism". The

Hebrew is literally, "Don't recognize faces." They are not to allow the fact that they are familiar with one party in the case to bias them – whether through family link, old school tie, or masonic covenant. A bribe blinds the eyes of the wise and twists the words of the innocent. If a judge accepts a bribe he is a law-breaker. He becomes a guilty criminal, and it is he who should be brought before the bar.

Bribes buy the right to do wrong.

A bribe will often buy the turning of a blind eye to evil. Was there ever a bribe asked for, offered, or taken, which was righteous? No, never, not one. The bribe is the currency of injustice.

I was deeply moved by an International Justice Mission video that presented an African man who had been kept in jail, though known to be innocent. He had been beaten repeatedly and tortured because the wicked perpetrators thought they would be paid a bribe by the victim's family in order to get him released. This is painfully all too common: arrest, imprisonment, and beating – all without charge – are used as a way to raise a bribe from relatives to buy the victim's release.

God hates bribery because God is compassionate – and bribery oppresses the poor. God hates bribery because he loves truth and justice. A bribe is an abuse of truth, whereas God is truth. God is *summum bonum,* ultimate goodness, so bribery is a form of idolatry, treating money rather than God as the most valuable thing. God lives for the other, whereas bribery is always for the self-interest of the bribed and the briber. Rabbi Dr Louis Jacobs writes:

> *The injunction against taking bribes has been applied in*
> *the Jewish tradition not only to the judge who allows gifts*
> *given to him to influence his decision but to every Jew*
> *who should not allow the prospect of gain to influence the*
> *pursuit of truth.*

Moses continues: "Justice, and only justice, you shall follow" (Deuteronomy 16:20a). The repetition makes God's will emphatic. The judge must not be influenced by any other factor than the justice in the immediate case presented to him; wider, pragmatic concerns, claims of the greater good, the benefit to a majority, may not be entertained.

The consequence of living justly is good living – "that you may live and inherit the land the Lord your God is giving you" (Deuteronomy 16:20b). The consequence of a society of bribery is that the land is defiled and the people destroyed. Whatever convergence of factors lies behind the current financial collapse in the West, I suspect we will find in the rubble a lot of greed and bribery!

2. Society often operates on the bribe

Tragically the bribe has entered every aspect of our society: the judiciary, the academy, the economy, politics, even the church.

Bribery in law

One only has to google the words "judiciary" and "corruption" to find it a global concern. English history is certainly littered with the debris of judges sacked for bribery. The famous scientist Francis Bacon, who became Lord Chancellor in 1618, later pleaded guilty to twenty-one charges of bribery and corruption, having accepted huge amounts from litigants to rule in their favour. He was fined £40,000 and sentenced to a term of imprisonment in the Tower of London. Bishop Hugh Latimer, the Oxford martyr, wrote of judges: "They all love bribes. Bribery is a kind of princely thieving." While a judge taking bribes would be almost unthinkable today, one has to ask about the actual process of appointment to the judiciary. Whether judges are appointed by their peers or by the presiding government, an office of such influence will be a target for abuse and corruption.

Bribery in the academy

Great pressure is brought to bear on academics, professors, and university institutions to welcome funding from companies, in order to pursue research that may have morally questionable results. This may be in the field of bio-ethics, drugs, cosmetics, or technology with military application. Money often compromises intellectual integrity.

A few years ago an Oxford college launched an investigation into allegations that some of its dons were prepared to offer to take below-standard students if parents pledged cash donations to secure their child's place.[27]

Bribery in economics

Throughout the world many economies function on the basis of the kickback: money or benefits paid as a bribe to secure a deal. There is the declared money on the table and the hidden money under the table. In some countries kickbacks may even be tax-deductible if declared on returns and shown to be necessary to secure the contract.

One of my hobbies is horology. A well-known watch brand has a waiting list of several years for certain stainless steel sports models. I have often read on watch forums that not a few unscrupulous jewellers will keep these desirable models in their safes. If asked for, they will sell it to you at the proper recommended retail price, but also suggest that you buy some

---

27 www.guardian.co.uk/uk/2002/mar/24/oxbridgeandelitism. highereducation

jewellery from their shop for your wife... to "guarantee we can get the watch for you".

It has been suggested that the cost of kickbacks and the corruption of bribery adds to the average value of goods purchased up to 15 per cent, totalling hundreds of billions of pounds. Is that "just business" or is it theft? The rich can afford to pay, and they are often powerful enough to escape paying. But it's the poor who can hardly afford to pay and who suffer through it. On a visit to Kenya President Obama and his film crew had to pay $1,000 dollars to Customs to allow their camera equipment through. He later complained to the president and got the money returned. The poor don't have the ear of presidents, or their power. They just get ripped off.

Bribery in politics

In the infamous "cash for questions" scandal MPs were given money to ask questions and represent the interests of others who were scheming and manipulating affairs so as to buy and use government for their own good. And then there is "cash for honours", that age-old system in Britain whereby the wealthy receive knighthoods or peerages by giving or lending huge sums to political parties. Nominees for honours are considered by the Honours Scrutiny Committee, set up in the 1920s after Prime Minister David Lloyd George was exposed for selling honours. But has this selling ever stopped? Or has it simply become less open? It has been claimed that under Margaret Thatcher a peerage cost £5 million in donations and a knighthood £1 million.

A similar misuse of the bribe in politics is seen in the USA, where they call it pork barrel politics (possibly because in the nineteenth century a barrel of pork was a sign of wealth). A politician in power spends millions on investing in their constituency – on hospitals, roads, schools and so on – so that they can later rely on the votes of those who benefit. The American statesman Joseph P. Kennedy said, "Don't buy a single vote more than necessary. I'll be damned if I'm going to pay for a landslide."

Major sporting events are often tainted with bribes – whether it's voting members of FIFA or the IOC, taking money to vote for certain countries to host the World Cup or the Olympic Games. The bribe appears to know no bounds.

Bribery in church

Sadly, the church has not been exempt from the love of money and power and has often been more interested in "storing up riches on earth" than in heaven. Pope Gregory VIII bribed the church by offering "indulgences" by the thousand to any who would help fund the Crusade or who themselves would travel to war in the Holy Land, in God's name, covering it in the blood of slain Jew and Saracen for the offer of forgiveness. Indeed, the Reformation was in part precipitated by a theological protest to the church's offering of salvation or early release from purgatory for monies paid. It was not just Judas who sold his soul for silver.

We can, of course, resist bribery. The Puritan Richard Baxter was offered the bishopric of Hereford to change his Reformed views and stop being such an irritant to the establishment. He could not be bought. The Puritan Thomas Manton was offered the Deanery of Rochester if he accepted the Act of Uniformity issued in 1662. He refused.

For centuries the church wed itself to the spirit of empire, legitimating and sanctioning its power plays and land grabs. Portugal and Spain's empires in South America, Britain's empire from sunrise to sunset – all jumped on the backs of self-interested powers in order to baptize a few more "natives" and extend their parishes (and God's kingdom!). But did they turn a blind eye to injustice? Did they give religious legitimation to oppression? Did their silence or even their sanction sometimes get bought? In Germany in the 1930s the so-called "German Christians" were so enamoured with Hitler's promise to make much of the church in his Third Reich, a gross parody of the messianic millennium reign, that Hitler stepped into power on the tide of the church's votes. They were bribed by the demonic for the price of a bishop's seat in Hitler's cabinet. Many were sincere, idealized Nazis, but many others quickly realized they had been duped.

3. The bribe is the currency of the demonic

Ultimately the devil is the great briber – self-interested, manipulating, and perverting the good. The devil sought to bribe Christ, deflecting him from obedience to his Father, by offering him all the kingdoms of world (Matthew 4:8–9). The devil was behind the Pharisees who bribed Judas to betray Jesus with thirty pieces of silver (Matthew 26:14–15). The devil bribed Pilate who, fearing riots in the hot-bed of Passover in Jerusalem, washed his hands and turned a blind eye to Christ being crucified. The devil was behind the Jewish authorities who bribed the Roman guards to say the body of Jesus had been stolen (Matthew 28:12–15). Ultimately, of course, his bribe backfired – Christ is the victim of bribery and yet, ironically, he became payment for our unrighteousness.

Satan the briber is undone by his bribery. The devil was behind Governor Felix who kept Paul imprisoned for two years, hindering the advance of the gospel work going into Europe as Paul planned. He did this hoping to gain a bribe for his release (Acts 24:26). Again, the briber is undone, because in the two years he is in prison Paul is able to write the bulk of his New Testament epistles, which have helped the cause of Christ and built the church for two millennia. Some have suggested the devil was behind Constantine bribing the church into becoming the official religion of Rome in the fourth century, as once she was bribed she was no longer able to be prophetic but, now wed to state and politics, she became compromised, growing fat and self-indulgent. Bought for the price of no more persecution, a seat at the table of social power, a purple shirt and a purple ring for the bishops – both the hallmark symbols of a Roman magistrate.

And oh, how the devil has bribed humanity since the garden of Eden, offering the world what God had already given her in creation. Adam and Eve were made in God's image, and yet the devil offered them the chance to be "like God". They were bribed with the promise of nothing. Not much of an exchange: a lost eternity for a momentary mouthful of fig. Pandora's box was opened, all hell let loose, and heaven lost. And still today the devil whispers and offers us pleasure, satisfaction, prosperity, power, if only we take the trade. The day I handed in my notice to go and serve God, living by faith as an evangelist, I was offered a double promotion and a large pay rise. Was that not the demonic seeking to buy me off serving God – all for "a mess of pottage" (Genesis 25:29–34 KJV)?

How can we as a church respond? We must discern the demonic spirit behind the bribe. We must be attentive to the dark powers that would buy us to rob us. We need courage and honesty to speak up and speak out for those who are victims of bribery. We need to recognize the love of money as often the root of bribery. We need to live in the opposite spirit, giving to the poor who cannot repay – as Christ said, inviting for a meal those who cannot invite us back (Luke 14:12–14). We won't take bribes, we won't pay bribes. We will be people of integrity.

The Bible says we were bought at a price. That price was God's beloved Son. May we never sell out.

Chapter 8

Amazing Grace

'Twas grace that taught my heart to fear, and grace my fears relieved. [28]
John Newton

The whole world loved Mother Teresa, and long before she was awarded the Nobel Peace Prize, and before the Pope beatified her to make her a "church saint", we all knew she was a saint. Tough, gritty, no-nonsense Albanian nun, who didn't suffer fools gladly, she became an icon of grace, willing to leave her home and go to the 400,000 street dwellers – among the poorest, most deprived, most pathetic people in the world. They were the social outcasts of a religious system whose principle of cyclic cause and effect said to the lowest caste, the untouchables: "It's your mess; you clean it up." Which is why, when Mother Teresa began her work, some Hindu scholars tried to stop her on the grounds that she was interfering in the karmic cycle! While many Indians loved her as their national hero, some extremist Hindus hated her and threatened to burn down her hospital.

What made her so gracious? The fact she had glimpsed God's grace

Many people, Western and Eastern, couldn't comprehend how Mother Teresa could stomach embracing people from the street

---

28 From the hymn "Amazing Grace" (1779).

who were half-eaten by rats, their wounds filled with maggots and running with pus. She would pray, bathe their wounds, bandage them and let them die with dignity. She could do it because she understood these literally rotten beggars to be loved by Jesus every bit as much as she was. And when they often died shortly after, they could say thankfully: "I have lived all my life like an animal; now I am dying like an angel."[29]

The Scottish theologian James Stewart was fond of describing God's work as alchemy[30] – a loving mercy and grace that transforms the base into the beautiful! C. S. Lewis once attended a debate discussing the religions and the uniqueness of Christianity. All the major religions had conceptions of divinity, sacred scriptures, sacrifices for sin, calls to holy living, deeds of mercy, prayers, and devotions. But what was the unique contribution of Christianity? C. S. Lewis stepped in: "Oh that's easy: grace."[31] This is the distinctive feature of Christianity – contrary to popular perception, God is not a petty minded accountant with a debit/credit ledger totting up good deeds and bad deeds, because through Christ it's all credit; he seeks to deposit mercy, grace, forgiveness, sonship, and royal inheritance into our account!

The word "grace" comes from the Greek *charis* meaning favour, gift, goodwill. The root *char* means well-being, and *chara*, "joy", is related to it. In classical Greek it was used of the benevolence demonstrated to people by the gods. Our English term "charmed" comes directly from it – meaning blessed, favoured, fortunate. Grace is gratis – free, unmerited, unwarranted, underserved, a gift. And this defines the nature of God and his actions toward humankind. It must therefore become the hallmark of the church's relationship to the world.

29 Mother Teresa told this story as she gave a speech on receiving the Nobel Peace Prize in 1979.
30 *The Heralds of God*, p. 160.
31 Quoted in Philip Yancey, *What's So Amazing About Grace?*, p. 45.

1. The place of grace

Grace is like a watermark found on every page of the Bible. Grace is the fingerprint of God, traceable in all his dealings with humanity. No one has understood Christianity, no one has understood the nature of God, no one has understood the Bible, who hasn't understood grace. But that which is the *métier* of divinity is so often alien to humanity, and so we often find it difficult to be grasped by grace, and to generate grace. Grace is all over the place in the record of God's dealings with humankind in Scripture – the specific word occurs over 150 times, and its related Hebrew word *chesed* over 300 times. But it's not just the word. Semantics aside, the concept appears in all God's doings. The whole of the believer's life is formed, fashioned and framed by grace. Grace is not an extra, a supplement to the regular diet. Grace is Christianity – we begin, continue and end with grace.

The apostle Paul said we are chosen by grace (Romans 11:5); called by grace (1 Corinthians 3:10); saved by grace (Titus 2:11); justified by grace (Romans 3:24); receive a gospel of grace (Acts 20:24); enabled to approach the throne of grace (Hebrews 4:16); continue through grace (Acts 13:43); are sustained by grace (2 Corinthians 12:9); live in the age of grace (Ephesians 3:2) under the reign of grace (Romans 5:21). Paul often gets a bad press in some more liberal church quarters, where he has been interpreted as a rather mean-spirited, critical, smug, former Pharisee pushing his weight around, in particular with regard to women. Not so. Paul was the Apostle of Grace – in the thirteen letters he wrote, every single one begins with grace and ends with grace, with a commendation and a prayer that his readers might enjoy the gift of grace from Christ. For Paul, no doctrine can be understood, and no ethic of the Christian life can be lived, apart from the milieu of grace. Our religion is grace from start to finish.

Grace is the hallmark of the person and work of Jesus. In John's Gospel we read that Jesus came "full of grace and truth" (John 1:14). This thought is then repeated in verse 17 where "grace and truth came through Jesus". In verse 16 we have a diamond of a verse, which the NIV translates as "one blessing after another". A more accurate rendering would be: "From his fullness we have all received grace upon grace." That's grace followed by more grace. When I was a difficult and demanding teenager, my mother in exasperation would sometimes say to me, "It's just one thing after another with you!" She meant one problem after another, one crisis after another, one demand after another. With Jesus it's one good thing after another – free gift, goodness, favour. God's grace flows from his being. He is the gracious one. As the sea's waves lap against the shore, day in, day out, regardless of weather, barrier, or bather, so God's grace just keeps coming – grace upon grace!

2. The face of grace

God's command to Adam and Eve not to eat of the tree of knowledge of good and evil was not about restriction but compassion. God did not want them to die; he did not want a rupture to come into their relationship with him and with each other. And even after they ate and in their shame hid from him, he drew them out, wooing them and replacing their garments of shame with animal skins. Yes, they had to be expelled from Eden, but God left Eden as well and accompanied them. The whole of Scripture may be seen as God journeying with humankind, seeking to return them to the paradise lost.

I once heard someone say that the biblical story of Noah revealed a God who was malicious and capricious, a vengeful divine destroyer, obliterating life by flood. On the contrary, this ancient story is of grace before judgment. For 120 years (Genesis 6:3), throughout the sinfulness and rebellion of humanity, God showed grace and restraint, not breaking out in judgment, but coming in mercy. The apostle Peter wrote that "God's patience waited in the days of Noah, while the ark was being prepared" (1 Peter 3:20), calling Noah "a herald of righteousness" (2 Peter 2:5). For that 120 years, as Noah made the ark, he preached God's righteousness and human sinfulness and the need for repentance. And he had a massive visual aid! I believe the ark need never have been used and the flood need never have come. It could have lain there and rotted. But tragically, after 120 years of grace and preaching and mercy before judgment, no one beyond Noah's family responded, and the floods came.

In the book of Exodus we see the Israelites breaking their backs, making bricks without straw for their oppressive master (Exodus 5:16). Grace is to be found in God's deliverance, providing for them for forty years as they wander through the desert, feeding them with manna from heaven and water from rock, not allowing their shoes to wear out. Grace is also in the list of tabernacle furnishings in Exodus, establishing a place of grace where a holy God could meet and minister and remain with Israel. Grace is in the whole sacrificial system in Leviticus, each sacrifice a means for finding God or responding to him after he has so graciously provided for and protected Israel. Grace is in the year of Jubilee, when every fifty years all debts were to be cancelled, all slaves freed. Grace is in the command not to harvest to the edge of the field but leave the gleanings for the poor. Grace is in the gift of the land promised to Abraham, a land of "great and good cities that you did not build, and houses full of all good things that you did not fill, and cisterns that you did not dig, and vineyards and olive trees that you did not plant" (Deuteronomy 6:10–11). That's the nature of grace!

John said Jesus pre-eminently personifies grace – he is full of it!

When he said "follow me" we see grace, offering an invitation to be with God. When he said "feed them" we see grace, not wanting 5,000 to go hungry. When he said "forgiven are your sins" to the cripple, we see grace making a way for healing. When he said "fear not" to the terrified twelve on the boat, we see grace preceding storm-stilling power. When he said "fetch him" and they brought blind Bartimaeus, we see grace heeding the cry of the needy. When he said "friend" to Judas as he came to betray him with a kiss, we see grace. When he said "faith has saved you" to the woman who wiped her tears off his feet with her hair, we see grace to wipe away sin. When he said "Father forgive them" as they killed him on a tree, we see grace, what the apostle Paul called "the immeasurable riches of his grace in kindness toward us in Christ Jesus. For by grace you have been saved through faith" (Ephesians 2:7–8). Grace is the colour of blood. It was grace that sent Jesus to the cross, grace that kept him on the cross, grace that poured from his wounds. Grace is the weight of the world's sin on Christ's shoulders. Rightly says the mnemonic that G-R-A-C-E is God's Riches At Christ's Expense.

Robert Capon once claimed the lesson of the Reformation was: "God saves us single-handedly."[32] God revealed this to Martin Luther, whose emaciated body from long fastings, his back scarred from self-flagellation, his knees bloody from walking up the steps of Santa Scala, didn't impress God one jot – in fact it offended God, because it suggested Jesus' death was not up to the job of forgiving sinners. But Luther discovered that salvation is by grace alone, through faith alone, in Christ alone. The dying words of Jonathan Allen of the Salvation Army were, "I deserve to be in hell, but God interfered." Surely we deserve

32 Robert Farrar Capon, *Between Noon and Three*, pp. 114–15.

hell for our sin and rebellion against God, but God interfered; love interfered; Christ interfered; grace interfered.

3. The waste of grace

When we come to the Lord's table we eat the bread and drink the wine, symbols of Christ's sacrifice and a feast that, according to the Thirty-Nine Articles, is a "means of grace", a mediator of divine grace. What a blasphemy it would be if this grace, handed to us on a plate and chalice, were to be spat back in Jesus' face! Yet I wonder sometimes if that is not what we do, either through our licence or through our legalism.

Licence takes grace for granted. Paul repeatedly said that we were not to "sin that grace may abound" (Romans 6:1). We are not to continue in sin just because God is so gracious that he will be bound to forgive us. Imagine if the prodigal son, having returned and been welcomed and forgiven, and robed and ringed, went off and pawned the fine robe and ring to squander it again on sin, knowing his father is a soft touch and will always forgive him and bail him out. This was the problem in Corinth. They thought they understood grace and felt they could simply and wilfully continue in their immorality, injustice, and idolatry! They took grace for granted.

This is all too present in the church, as Christians continue to live like the unconverted, with no fear of God and a belief in what Dietrich Bonhoeffer termed "cheap grace" (in his classic book *The Cost of Discipleship*). But just as prevalent is legalism, the proud refusal to accept a free handout. This is the religious person who thinks they can give God a hand. Legalism stems from a lack of confidence in God's forgiveness, or from an independence or arrogance in which we desire to justify ourselves by our works, to give us something to boast about. This was pre-eminently displayed in the Galatian church – that thought that grace needed supplementing with the loss of their foreskins! Paul said this graceless, law-driven church was bewitched (Galatians 3:1). They had placed themselves in bondage (5:1). They were joyless (4:15), had become judgmental (5:15), and would receive judgment (3:10).

The inability to receive grace creates an inability to be gracious. One reason this is so tragic is because the legalist who cannot receive God's grace will not permit others to receive grace. The one whose hand is open to receive grace has a hand open to give away grace. Those who are close-fisted to God's amazing handout are invariably tight-fisted in demonstrating grace. We see this clearly in the older brother syndrome in the story of the prodigal son (Luke 15:25–32). He is wound so tight, and so independent of his father's grace, that he profoundly resents his brother returning and getting a royal welcome. He refuses to celebrate and embrace his brother and party with the rest. Instead he feels sore that he has never had a goat for a party, let alone a fatted calf. The elder brother's mindset is "I have *slaved* for you all these years," while the pained father retorts, "Son, all I have is yours." But the older brother has never availed himself of his father's grace, and is so bitter inside, so debit/credit minded, that he cannot stomach grace being given to his wayward brother.

If we are to be those whose lives are marked by justice and mercy, if we are to be able to give away amazing grace, graciously, freely, without expecting return or reward, then we will need to learn to live by grace, and that starts by receiving it joyfully.

God's graced people are God's gracious people

We need to embrace the grace of God and then extend the grace of God. Why have I written a whole chapter on the nature of grace and our experience of grace? What has this to do with our themes of justice and mercy? Just this: justice and mercy flow from grace. The nature of divine being and the structure of all divine action is grace. To put it more technically, grace is a primary predicate of divinity.

Paul wrote that we his people are called to be "imitators of God, as beloved children", living a life of love, "as Christ loved us and gave himself up for us, a fragrant offering and sacrifice to God" (Ephesians 5:1–2). Having experienced his love and grace, we are to imitate them, giving ourselves to the world. That will be an acceptable offering to God. As God's people we are to reflect his nature, do his works, and so mediate him to the world. God's people are the grace people. But we must be grasped by grace ourselves if we are to bestow it on others. The famous Swiss theologian Karl Barth said: "By this shall you be judged: did you live by grace?" And I would add, by this shall you be judged, did you live graciously?

Chapter 9
Filled with Tenderness

Still let him prompt the unlettered villagers
To tender offices and pensive thoughts.[33]
William Wordsworth

C. S. Lewis once wrote that cats were the Pharisees of the animal kingdom,[34] but in 2010 the world had a tsunami wave of tenderness toward a cat that was deliberately placed by a woman in a wheelie bin and left there for twelve hours, until the deed was picked up on a review of CCTV footage. This incident made headlines in all the national newspapers, TV and radio news, even reaching New Zealand! One questions whether such tenderness for a cat was matched by equal tenderness and protest at the 20 million who were displaced by Pakistan's floods at the same time. Living justly and mercifully is living with a tender heart. The hard-hearted cannot heal or be healed.

Rempli de tendresse

Christian stateswoman and survivor of Auschwitz, Corrie ten Boom, recalled a remarkable revelation she received when she was a prisoner in Ravensbruck Concentration camp.[35] Her sister

---

33 From the poem "The Old Cumberland Beggar". Retrieved from http://rpo.library.utoronto.ca/poem/2353.html
34 *Letters to an American Lady* (she was Mary Willis Shelburne), 21 March 1955, p. 40.
35 This story is told in Corrie ten Boom, *A Prisoner and Yet*, p. 134.

Betsie was ill in the camp's so-called hospital ward, which was little more than a room with beds where the sick were dumped. Betsie lay sick sharing a bed with a psychotic French girl who would bite and punch the elderly and frail Betsie and push her out of the bed. Repeatedly Betsie would climb back into bed, gentle and kind, without complaint or criticism, and seek to share Christ's love with this tormented girl.

Corrie, watching this, was furious. She shouted at God, blaming him for her sister's predicament and asking him how he could allow such a thing to occur – if being a political prisoner and labourer in Auschwitz wasn't bad enough, Betsie had to endure the assaults of a deranged French girl! Suddenly, Corrie heard an audible voice speaking to her in French. It was so clear she actually swung round expecting to see someone. But there was no one – it was God speaking. He said, "*Rempli de tendresse* – filled with tenderness." God answered Corrie's pained questioning, and he did so in the language of this needy little French lass. God had placed Betsie next to her as his envoy, to care and show grace and mercy and tenderness and love to this tormented creature. Filled with tenderness: that's why Betsie was there; that's what she was giving, and that's what the French girl was receiving. She was never going to experience tenderness unless someone filled with divine tenderness could see beyond her aggression. And, despite Corrie's anger toward both God and the girl, God was speaking tenderness to Corrie as well.

The word "tenderness" in fact comes from the Old French language, where it meant "to stretch toward". So it implies a grace-filled stretch that reaches out, a movement in the direction of someone in sympathy, empathy, charity, and love.

You do not have to look below the surface to see our world is full of pain and shame, blighted by fears and tears and wounded years, longing for tenderness. Sing about tenderness and you will always have listeners: among the best-selling pop songs of all time are Elvis Presley's "Love Me Tender" and Otis Reading's "Try a Little Tenderness", while Blur offered "Tender". These songs, with their lyrics and their longing, resonate with the deep desire in the human heart. The demands of twenty-first-century life bring a deep-seated angst born out of insecurity and unbelonging. So many are born to single mums with a gnawing need for community, rejection filling their souls from infancy. Meanwhile the epidemic of divorce continues, as the constant mobility for work breaks down community life. As for the interface with screens and online networks, many are still learning that what these have to offer is more pseudo-community than real.

Offering to fill the void of intimacy, the demonic world of internet pornography crouches behind the screens – cyber-stimulation and momentary endorphin release, but another stone of shame deposited to carry in your soul, making it even less likely you'll ever enjoy true intimacy with your spouse or indeed with God. The increase in sexual addiction, sexual perversion, promiscuity, marital infidelity, is not simply the "increase in wickedness", but I suspect a crisis of brokenness and a desperate search for tenderness. How many of those trapped in sexual sin whom I have counselled and prayed with over the years, are simply desperate to give momentary relief to a deep and haunting sense of rejection?

1. Tender-heartedness is divine likeness

The apostle Paul writes: "Be kind to one another, tenderhearted, forgiving one another, as God in Christ forgave you. Therefore be imitators of God..." (Ephesians 4:32 – 5:1).

Tenderness is divine likeness. The Oxford intellectual and social theorist, John Ruskin, once observed, "An infinitude of tenderness is the chief gift and inheritance of all truly great men."[36] If they possess that gift, they are indeed great, but only because they imitate a great God. The word translated "tenderhearted" in the ESV is rendered in other English versions as "compassionate". The Greek word is *eusplagchnos*, which referred to the bowels, or inner organs that were regarded by the ancients as the centre of feelings. This sense is reflected in our modern idiom which speaks of our "heart going out" to someone. And James gave us an extraordinary description: "The Lord is *polysplagchnos*" – literally "with many tender hearts" (James 5:11).

God is often misrepresented as distant and vengeful, both malicious and capricious, especially in the Old Testament. How wrong this blasphemous notion is. On the contrary, we see a tender-hearted God who is always going out of his way to forgive, to restore, and to be merciful to a repeatedly rebellious Israel.

The Jewish scholar Abraham Heschel wrote, "God's prophets proclaimed a pathetic theology." Here "pathetic" is used in its original meaning as "full of pathos or feeling". Yes, the prophets revealed a *feeling* God, one of "intimate concern".[37] Consider the prophet Isaiah who expressed God's gracious heart as one who "weeps" for Jazer and "drenches" Heshbon "with tears" (Isaiah 16:9). But here's the amazing thing: these were Israel's sworn enemies. So why was God weeping over them? Because they were unrepentant, and so God in his righteousness must break out against them in judgment and destruction – but not without weeping at their wasting of his grace.

Or consider God's tender-hearted words to Israel: "Comfort, comfort my people, says your God. Speak tenderly to Jerusalem, and cry to her that her warfare is ended, that her iniquity is pardoned" (Isaiah 40:1–2). The Hebrew translated "speak tenderly" is a Hebraism which literally means "speak to the

36 John Ruskin, *The Two Paths*, p. 18.
37 Abraham Heschel, *The Prophets*, p. 241.

heart": the prophet was to speak comfort to the heart of God's people, from heart to heart. The Edwardian Cambridge minister P. T. Forsyth, in correcting people's misunderstanding of God's nature, wrote:

> *The holiness of God is the holiness of love... It is, indeed, infinite tenderness; but it is soul tenderness, it is moral tenderness, it is atoning, redeeming tenderness. It is the tenderness of the Holy, which does not soothe but save.*[38]

Even God's fearful holiness is tender-hearted.

Pre-eminently we see tireless tenderness in Jesus Christ. I have often visited France and Spain on holiday. As I go sightseeing around the churches, I see many filled with kitsch, pale, chipped, bisque statues of Jesus, revealing a large exposed red heart – generally known as the "sacred heart". This mystic devotion and cult of meditation on Jesus' heart took off in the context of the bloodletting and arid secularism of the French Revolution, and revived a century later during the visceral violence of the Franco-Prussian War. At just the point when religion was being exorcized from France and countless lives were being lost in revolution, and at just at the point when Spain and France were locked in bloodletting, the people turned to God, away from barricades and bayonets, to hide themselves in God's heart. In a world marked by trauma, some tenderness is found meditating on the heart of Jesus. The statues may seem vulgar and in poor taste, but the sentiment, the longing, the theology, is profound: in a heartless world, Jesus' heart beats tenderly.

There is an inextricable link between Christ's tenderness and the miraculous. We hear so much teaching in the church on healing, signs and wonders, yet I never hear mention of tenderness and I never see signs of the miraculous. And I do wonder whether,

---

38 P. T. Forsyth, *Missions in State and Church*, p. 233.

if we had the heart of Jesus, we would see the hand of Jesus. Christ felt tender-hearted compassion for the "harassed and helpless" crowds, and exhorted his followers to "pray earnestly to the Lord … to send out labourers into his harvest" (Matthew 9:36–38). Seeing the great crowd, he felt tender-hearted love for them and healed them, before feeding over five thousand (Matthew 14:14–21). Moved with tender-hearted compassion on seeing two blind men, Jesus healed them (Matthew 20:34). Jesus saw a leper and, moved with tender-heartedness, reached out and touched him and healed him (Mark 1:41). When he saw a widow at Nain burying her only son, with no family to support her, Jesus was moved with tender-hearted compassion and raised the boy (Luke 7:13–15). What is indisputable is that Jesus' miracles were precipitated by tenderness, compassion, and mercy. They were not simply displays of power, wonders attesting to his divinity. First and foremost they were displays of his heart. Interestingly, with perhaps the two exceptions of the rich young ruler and Nicodemus, the Gospels don't portray those who came to Jesus doing so with great intellectual, existential, or theological questions. Rather, they are life's bruised reeds – the hungry, outcasts, broken, rejected, sinful, sick – and they came because they had nowhere else to go, and they knew he would receive them (John 6:68).

Pre-eminently Jesus' tender mercy stands out at his arrest, when he says to Judas the betrayer, "Friend, do what you have to do." He calls him friend, not enemy, not betrayer, and he does not scorn nor spit his words out – they are tender even in this dark night of knives. And he lets Judas kiss him. At the cross, in the throes of agony, shortly before he himself will be cut off from his earthly mother and his heavenly Father, he is thoughtful of the practical needs of Mary and John: "Dear woman, behold your son." While dying for the sins of the world, he is numbered with sinners and turns to the criminal who acknowledges him,

Filled with Tenderness

and offers tender hope: "Today you will be with me in paradise."
As he breathes his last he tenderly prays for those who have just
crucified him, those soldiers standing below who have driven
nails through his hands and feet. No threats or curses are heard,
just tenderness: "Father, forgive them, for they know not what
they do" (Luke 23:34). It was not the nails that held him there,
it was love. At the cross his tender heart is freely offered and
crushed to pay the penalty for our corrupt heart. He dies in our
stead so we can stand in his.

Billy Graham once visited Mother Teresa ministering in
the slums of Calcutta. He asked her what fired her compassion.
Saying nothing, saying everything, she merely pointed to the
crucifix on the wall.

2. Even as God is tender, so let us imitate him

Paul wants tenderness to be a hallmark of all children of God –
"be tenderhearted...be imitators of God" (Ephesians 4:32 – 5:1).
The first-century martyr Polycarp specifically lists tenderness
as a pre-requisite for deacons and bishops. It was certainly the
mark of one distinguished cardinal, Henri De Lubac. On one
occasion Pope John Paul II was giving a lecture when he saw
the aged priest De Lubac sitting in the congregation. The Pope
paused from his speech, and said, "I bow my head to Father
De Lubac." Who was this little known priest who could be
honoured so publicly and dramatically by the Pope? De Lubac
was a little-known French theologian who had humbly served
God, his church and his nation for decades. But he *was* known
for his kindness, what someone called "a genius for friendship",
and all who were privileged to be taught by him honoured him.
He understood this and expressed it in a life of long tenderness.

He once wrote:

> *One need not blush or excuse oneself for being tender: it is*
> *an honour for which one must be proud, it is a grace that*
> *one must spread, for where there is no tenderness, neither is*
> *there joy given nor joy received. I know of course that one*
> *can misuse one's heart, one can wither one's body and soul*
> *in debilitating and sterile tenderness. It is the path that is*
> *opened wide to those entering into life...It is the same with*
> *human tenderness as with all beautiful things: it must gain*
> *mastery over itself and free itself from its masks, just like the*
> *morning sun, leaving the mists of dawn...But one would be*
> *wrong to laugh at this word and this thing called affection. Do*
> *you think that the hearts of the great apostles did not overflow*
> *with this tenderness? Look again at the epistles of Saint Paul*
> *or at that wonderful passage from Acts that recounts the*
> *farewell of the saint to his faithful at Ephesus: tears stream on*
> *all sides from these eyes that will never see each other again*
> *here below. Meditate especially on the profound tones, the*
> *ardent rhythm of Paul, writing to his faithful, whom he has*
> *engendered in Christ and who are his children.*[39]

Where did De Lubac learn these tones of tenderness? Biographically he recalls: "My parents were hardly well-to-do...but we were bathed in tenderness."[40] De Lubac could be tender because he was nurtured in tenderness. And so we too, as children of God bathed in divine tenderness, are to exhibit this in all we do and with all whom we have to do. Paul makes it a necessary hallmark of all who follow Jesus.

---

39 I am quoting from Professor Maggie Dawn's blog, having been unable to locate the original source – http://maggiedawn.com/try-a-little-tenderness/
40 In Rudolph Voderholzer, *Meet Henri De Lubac*, p. 26.

Tender-hearted in our interactions with others

On numerous occasions when I've had that gnawing angst only a preacher knows, who has to deliver a sermon but has nothing to say, I have rung my dad for advice and he has answered: "Preach to broken hearts." There are always broken hearts out there, and God wants to bind them up. Jesus the tender-hearted came to "bind up the brokenhearted" (Isaiah 61:1).

Not so long ago a dear friend of mine saw his marriage collapse, despite months of counselling and prayer. He lost his family and his job. I drove to see him, going over in my head how I was going to tell him about his responsibilities to God, to church, to his family; how I was going to talk about the shame he had brought on himself and the pain he had brought on his family. I was up for a fight. But as I drove to him, rehearsing my lines, God loudly whispered to me, "Listen to him." Don't shout, don't criticize or condemn, just listen. And so I did, and I found my friend hurting and broken. He already knew the theology and the texts, and at this moment tenderness was what the Lord wanted to give. God found it easier to give it to him than I did. God is slow to anger and rich in love – we so often get it the wrong way round.

Folk singer Iris DeMent wrote a song, "Easy's getting harder every day." It is. Life is hard; no one gets through it easily, as they struggle to be nice to their children, wife, husband, colleagues, a stranger on the train, an attendant at the supermarket checkout. When he was dying of cancer John Wimber, the founder of the Vineyard Church movement, gave a series of final addresses to all the Vineyard pastors worldwide. On one such occasion, when the throat cancer meant he could not speak for long, the sermon was essentially his characteristic no-nonsense wisdom distilled from years of pastoring pastors: "Love Jesus, play nice, keep your fingers out of the till and your zippers up." I later read this quoted on a Vineyard pastor's blog, and the person only recalled the "fingers out of the till and zippers up" instruction. Wimber's first two exhortations had been dropped, even though they were the most important: loving Jesus and being kind! The Victorian novelist George Eliot wrote: "When death comes, it is never our tenderness that we repent of, but our severity."

Tender-hearted in self-inspection

I do not want to make light of human sinfulness, but often within the evangelical tradition we are better at finding sin than we are at forgiving it. This is particularly true where we have inculcated a critical spirit that is quick to condemn. In Romans 8:3 Paul notes that "God sent his Son in the flesh to condemn *sin* in the flesh" (my italics) – the cross was not a condemnation of me, but of sin in me. And the cross was the great divine embrace, the yes of grace (2 Corinthians 1:20), the yes of forgiveness, which always trumps the no of sin, judgment, and exclusion.

Some years ago, a wise member of our congregation said to me: "I think you can be too harsh on yourself and this makes you at times too harsh on others." Ironically, I had always thought I was too soft and not robust enough in my challenge to sin in others and myself. But I began to see that she might be right. If we have failed to receive the tenderness shown to us, we will struggle to be tender toward others. If we are slow to receive forgiveness ourselves, we will be slow to give forgiveness. If we treat ourselves with legalistic judgmentalism, we will do so the same to others.

Jesus said the greatest commandment was to love God and to love our neighbour as ourselves. We will be unable to love God and unable to love our neighbour until we love ourselves. We will be unable to love ourselves until we know ourselves loved by the fierce affections of God. After Paul says we are to be tender-hearted and imitate God in the passage we have been exploring, he then adds that "as beloved children" we are to "walk in love, as Christ loved us" (Ephesians 5:1–2). We cannot be tender-hearted, walking in love, until we know we are God's beloved children, loved by Christ. And for that we need a revelation: Paul continues, "Christ loved us and gave himself up for us" (Ephesians 5:2).

The Catholic monk and spiritual writer, Brennan Manning, tells of a period in his life when he was broken with exhaustion and spiritual dryness in which he could only sense the absence of God. He took a retreat, and one day spent thirteen hours in silent prayer; at the end God broke in and spoke, "Live in the wisdom of accepted tenderness."[41] Manning realized he had been living out of duty and not delight, out of responsibility to God rather than intimacy with him. He learned a deep lesson: that we must live our life with God accepting the fact that he likes us, he cares for us, he really is for us... he really, really loves us.

Tender-hearted in devotion

We can be so busy with church stuff that we miss Christ. Like Martha, fussing around and preparing meals and meetings, we miss just sitting at the feet of the Lord and enjoying his tenderness. And Jesus himself longs for our tenderness. Jesus thrilled in the tender touch of a harlot who anointed his feet with nard and dried them with her hair, commenting, "She has done a beautiful thing to me" (Matthew 26:10), while he rebuked Simon the Pharisee for not sharing an appropriate intimacy with him: "You gave me no kiss... You did not anoint my head with oil" (Luke 7:45–46). You stayed at arm's length!

In the garden of Gethsemane Jesus was downhearted: his disciples slept while he agonized. "Could you not watch with

41 Brennan Manning, *Abba's Child*, p. 3.

me one hour?" (Matthew 26:40). The psalmist said, "Kiss the Son, lest he be angry" (Psalm 2:12) – Christ longs for that kiss. As the Beloved in the Song of Songs he cries to us to "come away" with him (Song 2:10) for we are his beloved and we have stolen his heart. But just as in marriage, tenderness can grow cold and the relationship become clinical or ritual, so it can be in our relationship with Jesus. And oh, how we need to rekindle the fire of love! How often do I lose the discipline of intimacy – allowing the Lord to be left out while I am about his work? I do not want to just snatch fleeting moments with the Lord, studying his word for talks and sermons but missing intimacy; I want to linger in his presence, to love and be loved. I know that without it I become hardened in my soul and hardened toward others. It is from that place of experienced tenderness with Christ that we can be filled with tenderness for a broken world.

Tender-hearted in intercession: pray wet prayers

We read in Hebrews 5:7 that during his earthly ministry Jesus "offered up prayers and supplications, with loud cries and tears". The shortest verse in Scripture is, "Jesus wept" – and people remarked, "See how he loved him!" (John 11:35–36). Jesus wept over friends who had died, and he wept over a Jerusalem that had died to God. The prophet Joel encourages us to "let the priests, the ministers of the Lord, weep" (Joel 2:17). Similarly the prophet Jeremiah inspires us: "Oh that my head were waters, and my eyes a fountain of tears, that I might weep day and night for the slain of the daughter of my people" (Jeremiah 9:1). The famous late-Victorian missionary to India, John "Praying" Hyde, sparked the so-called Sialkot Indian Revival through wet prayers that moved the hearts of all who witnessed them – and which moved God. One observer wrote of his praying: "How often in the prayer room he would break into tears over the sins of the world… pleading for them with sobs, dry choking sobs that showed the depths of his soul being stirred."[42]

That statesman of revival Leonard Ravenhill reminisced in a sermon:

> *I remember going down High Holborn in London a few years ago… well it is a few, twenty five I guess. A little lady was going to the mail box. There she was, very, very stooped and she shakily put her mail into the box; then she turned to go into a building. Somebody asked me, "Do you know who that is?" And I said, "Not the slightest idea." "That is the widow of Hugh Price Hughes," at one time the king of the Methodist pulpit in England. His daughter gave us a huge biography of her father. And she said, "When he came back on a Sunday night from the service, if no one had been saved, he would be inconsolable. You couldn't comfort him. He wouldn't eat, he wouldn't drink. He wouldn't even take his long coat off. He threw himself over his bed and he sobbed and he sobbed and he sobbed and said, 'Why? Why? Why?'"[43]*

Tears rarely come from crocodiles. Ask God to break your heart with the things that break his.

Tender-hearted in mission

Here is an amazing promise from the psalmist: "He who goes out weeping, bearing the seed for sowing, shall come home with shouts of joy, bringing his sheaves with him" (Psalm 126:6).

I have heard people speak of evangelism as if they are spiritual scalp-hunters out to "bag another one". I have heard

42 Quoted in Francis McGaw's book *Praying Hyde – John Hyde's Prayer Life* http://www.calltoprayer.org.uk/encourager20.html
43 www.ravenhill.org/weeping1.htm

youthful evangelists speaking of personal evangelism as "hit-squadding". And the older term "soul-winning" conveys the sense of mission as sport, of a prize for a win. There is a desperate need in our mission work to be motivated not by an ought or a sense of sport but by compassion, tenderness, mercy, and love. It has often been remarked that people don't care what we know until they know that we care.

The American revivalist lawyer, Charles Finney, defined the third of his five signs of true revival as "Christians filled with tender burning love for souls". God is moved when his people are moved. The young David Brainerd coughed his lungs up with TB in the snowy wilderness, dying aged just twenty-eight. Why? For a life spent ministering the gospel to Native Americans. His diary is enough to stir even the coldest heart. One characteristic entry says this: "Felt some compassion for the Indians, but mourned I had not more." His tender heart brought an open heaven!

Have you ever asked God to fill your heart, to break your heart, with compassion and tenderness for someone, or some group? I promise you this: if you pray that sincerely, God will use you powerfully to draw them to Christ. He who goes out weeping, carrying seed to sow, will return with songs of joy bearing sheaves.

Soften my heart

How do we get a tender heart? In a former life before my ministry days I was in the meat industry, first as a butcher and then a wholesaler. In the meat trade tenderness is an all-important issue. Meat tenderness is influenced by a host of factors: genetics, diet, age, how stressed the beast is at slaughter, how long the carcass is hung, how it is butchered, how it is cooked. There are two ways to tenderize tough meat – bashing and marinating.

Bashing meat with a spiked mallet will crush the muscle fibres. Marinating is to soak the meat in wine, or oil, or lemon juice, which softens and separates the fibres. God wants a tender church, manifesting his tenderness to the world. And we get to choose. Either we can be bashed into tenderness and not bitterness, through the trials of life, praying with John Donne, "Batter my heart, three-personal God" embracing the exigencies that come our way and offering them to God to soften us up. Or we can marinate in God's love, becoming Spirit-softened saints.

I can always tell a Christian who is not Spirit-filled: they rarely laugh and they are not tender!

Chapter 10
Shut Your Mouth

And God said, "Let there be light," and there was light.
Genesis 1:3

A while ago I read an email from a man I deeply respected. In it he began by commending and encouraging a colleague's ministry. As I read it I thought: what a great bloke, what a man of God, writing so generously to encourage and affirm in this way. Then almost as an aside, the writer made a sharp dig at another friend and former colleague of mine. In an instant my opinion changed. What sort of a prize idiot is this, criticizing a friend of mine in an email? How dare he speak like that about my friend! Who does he think he is!

The minister's tongue one minute spoke blessing and the next cursing. And I likewise responded one minute by commending the writer, and the next I cursed him!

1. The shaming of the tongue

Throughout his epistle James uses the tongue as a diagnostic for spiritual health: "If anyone thinks he is religious and does not bridle his tongue but deceives his heart, this person's religion is worthless" (James 1:26).

I have a good friend who is a consultant pathologist in a large teaching hospital. For his MD thesis he wrote the definitive tome for dentists on the tongue. Dentists look at tongues all day long, because with one look at the tongue you can diagnose a large number of health issues and illnesses. The tongue reveals much about a person's physical state.

And the same is true for the spiritual state. The tongue is a spiritual barometer – not, as is believed in charismatic circles, through speaking in tongues, for Paul said that the gift of tongues is the least of the gifts. No, it is not God's gift of tongues that is the true test of spirituality, but how you use your own tongue as a gift. Sadly, it is perfectly possible to speak with the gift of tongues and then to use your speech to carp, criticize, and condemn others.

What's on your tongue shows what's in your heart. Jesus said, "It is not what goes into the mouth that defiles a person [food], but what comes out of the mouth [speech]" (Matthew 15:11). How many sins of the tongue can you come up with in a minute? Just consider the following, all of which come out of our mouth and condemn us as unclean in heart: complaining, grumbling, moaning, bullying, manipulating, double-entendre, coarse or smutty speech, jokes at someone's expense, lying, exaggerating, swearing, blaspheming, cursing, slandering, malicious talk, belittling, sarcasm, curt talk, condemning, cattiness, discouragement, boasting, insincerity… each is a foul-mouthed sin.

James teaches us about the negative power of the tongue. He begins, "Not many of you should become teachers, my brothers, for you know that we who teach will be judged with greater strictness" (James 3:1). Personally, as a teacher I have never liked that verse, much preferring Paul's comment that teaching elders deserve double pay (1 Timothy 5:17)! But James knows we will be judged on judgment day for every careless word uttered (Matthew 12:36). Those who preach and teach, especially for a living, have a lot more words to deliver – words that will influence widely, for good or for ill. How careful they must be that what they say they have first heard God speak to them.

The tongue is powerful

James tells us that the tongue is like a bridle, which, although tiny, can control a horse; or, just as a small rudder can direct a ship's course, so the tiny tongue can corrupt the whole body (James 3:3–4).

The tongue is among the smallest of muscles but it punches above its weight; its words and work shape worlds. What distinguishes humankind from animals, and enables us to have dominion over all animals, despite many being faster or stronger, is our capacity for "speech", that inherent rationality which enables us to create, to imagine, and then to communicate.

I believe it is our speech that specifically reflects our being created in God's image. God did not give animals creative speech. They have signals about food, sex, and danger, but not creative speech. God did not speak to the animals like Dr Doolittle did. There is no scripture where God talks to the animals. It was to humans that God gave speech, and with it the capacity to communicate with him directly. God's first task for humankind was to exercise rule by naming animals. Speech is power. In Jewish and Greek thought, words are efficacious, they actualize what they represent. In this sense words can create reality. To know the name of something is to have power over that something. God spoke the world into being. For good or ill, words have power.

The tongue is harmful

James tells us (3:5b–6) that, just as it takes only a small spark to cause a ravaging forest fire, so the tiny tongue can cause wholesale devastation.

One of Britain's greatest laws is the "freedom of speech", but this must always be tempered by laws against speech that incites violence and hatred. Sixty million people were killed in the Second World War, a war that in many respects was sparked and fuelled by Hitler's persuasive, mesmerizing, hate-filled speeches. Dark words and the dark hearts behind them have a lot to answer for.

The tongue can tear down. The old proverb "Stick and stones may break my bones but words will never hurt me" is simply untrue. Words can hurt more, cut deeper, take longer to heal than any physical assault. US president Benjamin Franklin said: "Man's tongue is soft, and bone doth lack; yet a stroke therewith may break a man's back." The Buddha said, "The tongue like a knife can kill, without drawing blood."

Sarcasm is a British staple, regarded and commended as a sign of quick wit. The term is a conjunction of two Greek words literally meaning "flesh-tearing". I have received many knocks and blows and the bruises and broken bones have healed quickly; yet words spoken over me still leave the soul tender decades on.

The tongue can be used to harm others, but James adds that the misuse of the tongue harms the person speaking, "corrupting the whole person" (James 3:6). The Greek term James uses is *spilousa* which means "staining". Foul words from the tongue don't simply go outward, they work retroactively, tainting our whole being... setting the whole course of our life on fire. Fire here is hinting at the future judgment and destruction of sin.

The tongue is capable of evil

The tongue is not intrinsically evil. I have already argued that the capacity for speech is good and an echo of God's nature. Speech was made good, for good, but James says it has been "set on fire by hell" (James 3:6). Speech, this gift of God that is intrinsic to the image of God in us, now bears the mark of sin. It is a "restless

109

evil" (verse 8), always looking to spew darkness, full of deadly poison like a venomous snake. The first time we meet the devil is in Genesis 3, who comes speaking, but already his words intend harm. Questioning God's word, undermining God's character, tempting God's children… his words are his tools to turn paradise into pandemonium. It is his words that work his evil – they always have. God's word creates, the devil's word destroys. The devil is called "the father of lies" (John 8:44) and "the accuser of our brethren" (Revelation 12:10 KJV), his words always working wickedness.

Paul says that a mark of sinful, fallen human nature is that we use our speech not for good but for evil. In Romans 3:13–14 he says of the unrighteous, "Their throat is an open grave; they use their tongues to deceive. The venom of asps is under their lips. Their mouth is full of curses and bitterness." Speech is often a signifier of sin. I am reminded of Tolkien's Grima Wormtongue in *The Lord of the Rings*. He feigned friendship, but his poisoned counsel turned King Theoden into a shrivelling shadow, rendering him impotent while Saruman built a demon army bent on destruction. Where are the whispering Wormtongues today in our press and political sphere, in pop music or literature, in the world of advertising or academies? Whose words beguile and bewitch?

The tongue is uncontrollable

James lists the four main categories of created beings from Genesis 1:26 – "beast and bird … reptile and sea creature" (James 3:7). He says that, while humanity can tame all these and exercise rule and dominion over them, "no human being can tame the tongue" (James 3:8) – literally, "not one human". Yet the devil is doing a good job using it as a bit to control us, as a rudder to direct us, and as a fire to harm us. No human of their own will and volition is able to control the tongue or resist the devil's controlling influence; only the spiritual man, submitted to God, can do this.

As I write, I recall a conversation I had this week over swearing. A colleague told me that a significant feature of his conversion was that he was once a foul-mouthed constant swearer, yet as soon as he was converted the Spirit controlled his tongue and he testifies to never swearing again. Not all have their tongue converted at conversion. It may not be swearing that is their misuse of it, but unclean jokes, or boasting, or snide comments, or harsh criticisms. The list goes on. Truly, we need our mouths as well as our souls to be washed out with the benefits of baptism.

The tongue is hypocritical

"With the tongue we praise our Lord and Father, and with it we curse men, who have been made in God's likeness" (James 3:9 NIV).

Some years ago I spoke at a university chapel service. The small choir sang the hymns of faith beautifully. Afterwards I sat with them at dinner and overheard a foul conversation about indecent sex, initiated by the choirmaster. It was so vivid and obscene that I can still recall what was said all those years ago. I'm no stranger to hearing people talk like that – but I was surprised to hear it immediately after worship from the supposed "worship leaders". I realized that many college choirs were made up not of sincere worshippers but people who like choral music, or who like the company, so I could not expect them all to be godly. However, the next year I was invited back to preach there and, as it happened, the set lectionary reading included God's rebuke: "This people honours me with their lips, but their heart is far from me" (Matthew 15:8). I preached and applied the text faithfully, speaking about hypocrisy and the need to live out what we sing out. I did not labour the point, or point the finger, for the text did its own work of teaching, correcting, reproving, and training in righteousness (2 Timothy 3:16). But a handful of choir members clearly did not like it. I guess they knew it had exposed their hypocrisy. They complained to the chaplain who duly wrote to tell me off. He did not think the choir needed preaching to.

Jesus once healed a man who was deaf and mute. Before he did so, the Gospel author records Jesus "sighed" (Mark 7:34) – the word indicates a deep sigh. Why was that? Perhaps it was because he knew that this man with his new ears would, having enjoyed blissful silence, now endure hearing words which would tear him apart, or with his restored speech he could now utter words which would hurt others. For Martin Luther, Jesus' sigh is a common sigh over all tongues and ears which speak or hear rotten words. Luther thought that the greatest harm inflicted on Christianity had not come from tyrants, but from that bit of flesh between the jaws.

2. The taming of the tongue

Having described the shaming of the tongue, we move to consider its taming. How can this wild fire be put out, or be directed away from evil toward good?

James has already said that not one man can tame the tongue, and that it's often controlled by Satan. Physically, the tongue is actually secured to the throat by a little horseshoe-shaped bone named the hyoid. James suggests that the spiritual root which controls the tongue is pride: "the tongue is a small member, yet it boasts of great things" (James 3:5). How often the misuse of the tongue is driven by pride, ego, an inflated view of ourselves, and a deflated view others, the flexing of a muscle to abuse others and to make ourselves look better. The American writer Emmet Fox stated, "Criticism is an indirect form of self-boasting."

Up to now James has been writing descriptively, but in chapter 4 he becomes prescriptive. Having reminded his readers that "God opposes the proud, but gives grace to the humble" (James 4:6), he then lists the following actions to help us overcome pride: submit to God, resist the devil, draw near to God, wash your hands, purify your hearts, grieve, mourn, weep, humble yourself.

Think before you speak...

...rather than speaking before you think. Most of the things I regret saying were said in a hurry – words spoken without forethought, rash and impetuous. There is wisdom in that old proverb about counting to ten before you reply. Solomon the wise wrote: "Even a fool who keeps silent is considered wise; when he closes his lips, he is deemed intelligent" (Proverbs 17:28). There is a useful acronym ENATA which offers a helpful filter for what comes out of our mouth. We ask ourselves of our speech the ENATA questions. Is what you are about to say Effective, Necessary, Accurate, Timely, and Appropriate? If not, then keep it to yourself.

Consider the impact of your words on people's feelings

Hal Chadwick, the popular actor from the eighties, once said, "No one so thoroughly appreciates the value of constructive criticism as the one who's giving it." As I write, I have been listening on the radio to Henry Winkler, the famous actor who starred as "The Fonz" in *Happy Days*, and who latterly has become a best-selling children's author. Throughout his school career he was profoundly dyslexic. He was made to feel stupid as he found it difficult to concentrate and keep up. He had a teacher who verbally abused him, crushing him and telling him he would never amount to anything. He is now an ambassador to countless schools in America and the UK where he encourages children to be all they can be. He was awarded an honorary

OBE by the Queen for services to special needs education. The message he gives all the schoolchildren is simple: you have a great gift inside you and your job is to discover it and give it to the waiting world.

Words change lives – for good or for ill. They can put heart in someone, or crush the heart out of someone. I read the tragic account of the trial of a gang who repeatedly used "threatening, abusive and insulting language" toward a mother and disabled daughter. Unable to take any more, and with no assistance from the authorities despite repeated cries for help, the mother got into her car with her daughter and set themselves on fire. Both died of their wounds.

There was a wartime poster that simply said, "Careless talk costs lives." Well, evil talk costs lives. What comes out of your mouth?

Remember your own imperfections before judging others

In one *Peanuts* strip Linus is holding his security blanket when he asks Lucy, "Why are you always so anxious to criticize me?" Lucy replies, "I just think I have a knack for seeing other people's faults." Linus responds, "What about your own faults?" Lucy answers, "I have a knack for overlooking those."

Perhaps if we were more accurately self-aware, we would be less hasty in judging others. Paul states: "For in passing judgment on another you condemn yourself, because you, the judge, practise the very same things" (Romans 2:1), and there is that old proverb that says: "Remember, when you point a finger at yourself, you have three pointing back at you." Shakespeare coined the now famous phrase "hoist by your own petard". A petard was a French bomb used to blow up doors and walls, and "hoist" is an old word for "raised" or "blown up". So we are blown up by our own explosive device – destroyed by the very thing we employed to destroy another. With the measure we judge we shall be judged. Jesus says that we ought to take the plank out of our own eye before we point out the speck in someone else's eye.

Remember that God will judge your every word

As we heard from James in the last chapter, words harm the hearer but they also harm the speaker. Scripture informs us that God's judgment is incurred by what we utter. In Numbers 12:8–10 Miriam and Aaron criticized Moses, and for their harsh words God struck them with leprosy! I have known people who were constantly swearing, criticizing, and attacking, and it seemed as if they aged with every dark word they uttered: another line was added, another frown deepened. Their faces gave away their mouth that gave away their heart.

But Jesus also warned there will be an ultimate final call to account for what comes out of our mouths, "every careless word" (Matthew 12:36). Every single word we ever uttered will go through God's divine spellcheck on judgment day! As each word is scrutinized we will be held accountable.

The rewards of godly speech

James offers us negative advice on how we speak followed by the positive: "do not speak evil against one another" (4:11), do not boast (4:16), "do not grumble" (5:9), "do not swear" (5:12), but rather "confess your sins to one another and pray for one another, that you may be healed" (5:16). When we speak ill, we become ill. But if our speech is righteous, if our speech confesses sin rather than commits sin, then when we pray for healing, healing will come. Perhaps there is so little healing in our prayers because there is so little well-being in our words. What comes out of our mouths is a tainted stream – cursing, carping and praying do not mix. The prophet Isaiah promised: "If you take away the yoke from your midst, the pointing of the finger, and speaking wickedness, if you pour yourself out for the hungry and satisfy the desire of the afflicted, then shall your light rise in the darkness and your gloom be as the noonday" (Isaiah 58:9–10). When we cease cursing others, we find God blessing us.

Be filled with the Spirit

"Be filled with the Spirit, addressing one another in psalms and hymns and spiritual songs" (Ephesians 5:18–19).

The Spirit is a speaking Spirit; Paul says by him we cry "Abba! Father!" (Romans 8:15) and "Jesus is Lord" (1 Corinthians 12:3). Before Peter was Spirit-filled at Pentecost he boasted, lied, and denied Jesus three times. After he was Spirit-filled he preached the gospel and saw thousands saved, and boldly stood for Christ before the authorities and the prospect of persecution. The evidence of a Spirit-filled person is in their speech – a tongue taken over by God, and used for God in prayer, praise, prophecy, or preaching. The Spirit may possibly set your tongue on fire with the gift of tongues, but he certainly will want you to gift him your tongue.

Consider giving words as gifts

In the classic 1970s Second World War movie *Kelly's Heroes*, the character Oddball (played by Donald Sutherland) says to Kelly (Clint Eastwood) when he brings worrying news of enemy activity: "Say something righteous and hopeful for a change." Just as we can all recall words spoken over us that have damaged our souls, we can also recall words spoken to us that changed our lives for the better. Whether it was encouragement, wisdom, blessing, or gratitude, words that built up and did not tear down made us better than we were.

We need to ask God to enable us to speak words that will change lives.

116

A little salt on the tongue

In Colossians 4:6 Paul instructs the church: "Let your speech be always gracious, seasoned with salt." Literally he says our speech is to be "always in grace". According to *Thayer's Greek Lectionary* the word for "grace", *charis*, is that which affords joy, pleasure, delight, sweetness, charm, loveliness. Our words should be such gifts to others. For this to occur, says Paul, our tongue needs to be "seasoned with salt". Ox tongues when they come out of cattle's heads are slimy, spiny, prickly, and full of poisonous toxins. But if they are salted in water, skinned and boiled, then they are a delicious delicacy. Let us ask God to season our tongue so that it might be purified, and that what comes out of it is full of grace, full of gifts, full of righteousness and mercy.

Solomon the wise has more to say about right and wrong use of speech than any other biblical author. I have listed below some of his proverbs, which reveal the consequence of the misuse of the tongue and the blessings of its right use. Here is royal wisdom that, if appropriated, will enable our lips to be marked by justice and mercy.

Proverbs 10:11

The mouth of the righteous is a fountain of life, but the mouth of the wicked conceals violence.

Proverbs 10:19–21

When words are many, transgression is not lacking, but whoever restrains his lips is prudent.

The tongue of the righteous is choice silver; the heart of the wicked is of little worth.

The lips of the righteous feed many, but fools die for lack of sense.

Proverbs 12:6

The words of the wicked lie in wait for blood, but the mouth of the upright delivers them.

Proverbs 12:14

From the fruit of his mouth a man is satisfied with good, and the work of a man's hands comes back to him.

Proverbs 12:18

There is one whose rash words are like sword thrusts, but the tongue of the wise brings healing.

Proverbs 12:19

Truthful lips endure forever, but a lying tongue is but for a moment.

Proverbs 12:22

Lying lips are an abomination to the Lord, but those who act faithfully are his delight.

Proverbs 12:25

Anxiety in a man's heart weighs him down, but a good word makes him glad.

Proverbs 13:3

Whoever guards his mouth preserves his life; he who opens wide his lips comes to ruin.

Proverbs 14:3

By the mouth of a fool comes a rod for his back, but the lips of the wise will preserve them.

Proverbs 14:7

Leave the presence of a fool, for there you do not meet words of knowledge.

Proverbs 15:1

A soft answer turns away wrath, but a harsh word stirs up anger.

Proverbs 15:2

The tongue of the wise commends knowledge, but the mouths of fools pour out folly.

Proverbs 15:4

A gentle tongue is a tree of life, but perverseness in it breaks the spirit.

Proverbs 15:28

The heart of the righteous ponders how to answer, but the mouth of the wicked pours out evil things.

Proverbs 15:31–32

The ear that listens to life-giving reproof will dwell among the wise.

Whoever ignores instruction despises himself, but he who listens to reproof gains intelligence.

Proverbs 16:23

The heart of the wise makes his speech judicious and adds persuasiveness to his lips.

Proverbs 17:4

An evildoer listens to wicked lips, and a liar gives ear to a mischievous tongue.

Proverbs 17:27

Whoever restrains his words has knowledge, and he who has a cool spirit is a man of understanding.

Proverbs 18:20–21

From the fruit of a man's mouth his stomach is satisfied; he is satisfied by the yield of his lips.

Death and life are in the power of the tongue, and those who love it will eat its fruits.

Proverbs 20:19

Whoever goes about slandering reveals secrets; therefore do not associate with a simple babbler.

Proverbs 24:28

Be not a witness against your neighbour without cause, or do not deceive with your lips.

Proverbs 25:11—12

A word fitly spoken is like apples of gold in a setting of silver.

Like a gold ring or an ornament of gold is a wise reprover to a listening ear.

Proverbs 26:24—25

Whoever hates disguises himself with his lips and harbours deceit in his heart;

when he speaks graciously, believe him not, for there are seven abominations in his heart.

Proverbs 28:23

Whoever rebukes a man will afterward find more favour than he who flatters with his tongue.

Chapter 11

A Royal Dog's Dinner

If we do not know ourselves to be full of pride, ambition, lust, weaknesses, misery and injustice, we are indeed blind. And if, knowing this, we do not desire deliverance, what can we say of a man?[44]
Blaise Pascal

The church is a mercy ministry of heaven. Through the church God extends his justice and mercy. One key area of mercy to which God called the church is in setting people free from slavery to the shadows and torments of evil. It was a hallmark of Jesus and the apostles, and it is a sign seen whenever God's kingdom comes.

I have called this chapter "A Royal Dog's Dinner". Mark 7:24–30 is not the easiest story in the Gospels to grasp. We see a woman willing to take from the hand of God what might be left for the dog, and on first reading you could be forgiven for inferring the very opposite of what the passage is actually intended to reveal.

The story must be interpreted in the context of the preceding section (Mark 7:1–23) where Jesus debates with the Pharisees over the true nature of what it means to be clean or unclean, pure, or defiled. The Pharisees made much of an outward display of ritual washings. They avoided "defiled" or "unclean" people and they rebuked Jesus for associating with the unclean "tax collectors and sinners" and for allowing his disciples to eat without washing

44 *Pensées*, Section VII, Morality and Doctrine, p. 450.

hands. Jesus countered this by rebuking them for their legalistic religious spirit which makes incidentals central and yet negates the true nature of the religion God requires, which is to act justly, love mercy, and walk humbly with God (see Micah 6:8).

Jesus shows (Mark 7:14–23) that it is not the hand but the heart that defiles a man, producing evil thoughts, immorality, and pride. The test of true religion is a clean heart and not clean hands. Obedience to God's law is not about ritual washings and right associations; it's not about hand washing but heart washing, and a heart that is pure will be a heart that moves the hand to reach out in mercy and deliverance to the poor and needy.

Mark illustrates this kingdom mercy, this "true religion", with the story of Jesus healing a pagan Gentile woman's demonized daughter. In verses 24–30 Jesus performs a prophetic act against the Pharisees' false notions of purity. His actions are as follows:

1. Jesus goes to Tyre, some twenty miles north of Capernaum. This was a Gentile area, and a former bitter enemy of Israel. By going abroad to rest and then minister, Jesus breaks scribal taboos, challenges the élitist, racist, exclusivist, separatist notion of the Pharisees' religion, and then reveals the universal reach of the love and mercy of God for Jew and Gentile alike.

2. Jesus enters a house here. Was it a Gentile house? It was a Gentile area, and there is no indication in the text that it is a Jewish home. No good Pharisee would ever enter a Gentile home. He would consider it unclean and therefore it would make him unclean.

3. Jesus engages in discourse with a Gentile woman. Again, no Pharisee and no rabbi would talk to even a Jewish woman (bar their mother, wife, or daughter) let alone engage in discourse with a pagan one. But remarkably this woman, whom the

Pharisee would regard as unworthy of a look let alone a conversation, receives the tender mercy of God, as she, and not the Pharisee, proves to be a model of true faith.

4. Jesus evicts an unclean spirit from a girl. Pharisees would think it was the pagan girl herself, in a pagan home, in a pagan nation that was unclean. But no, Jesus shows that it is the demon which defiles. He exorcizes the demon and the girl is left clean.

The irony is clear: the Pharisees, with all their religious activities, fail to recognize the coming of God in Christ and remain defiled; while a pagan mother recognizes Jesus as Lord, comes with humility, and receives mercy.

Let us explore this more closely.

1. Jesus was dog-tired

Jesus "arose and went away to the region of Tyre and Sidon. And he entered a house and did not want anyone to know" (verse 24).

This was essentially a desire for privacy, for time out from the pressures and demands of ministry and people. Jesus has been trying to make some space for himself and the twelve, but the crowds kept coming and Jesus was never one to turn anyone away, always responding to their desires and needs (Mark 6:30–34). But now he is exhausted from teaching, healing, and delivering, and he needs rest. He needs to recharge the batteries, refill the tank, and renew the vision.

The point is, even the merciful need mercy. There must be care for the carers. Jesus was not some kind of idealized Superman; he was real man, a whole man, who felt keenly the strains and frailties of humanity. He knew what it was to be exhausted, tempted, frightened, sexually attracted, lonely, misunderstood, disappointed, anxious, fearful, sad. As Martin Luther once said: "He was just like you and me, except he was God's Son and sinless." Jesus wept real tears, sweated real sweat, dripped real blood. Indeed, it is because he became "dust" that he can remember we are but dust. It is because he walked in our shoes, in our very flesh, that he knows what we are made of. He knows our weaknesses because he experienced them first hand, and his heart can be moved with compassion and mercy toward us. Tired like us, no longer tired with us, never tired of us.

How often we have failed to understand the so-called two natures of Jesus – as the creeds affirm, "truly God and truly man". Instead we end up with some halfway human who is neither fully God nor fully man, a Gnostic demi-divine. There was an early church heresy called docetism (from the Greek *dokeo* "to appear"), which asserted that Jesus only appeared to be human, for divinity could not possibly condescend and walk as we walked. They claimed that when Jesus walked on the sandy shores he left no footprint! What rot. The Church Fathers rightly responded, "That which is not assumed cannot be healed." That is to say, if Jesus didn't take on (assume) our humanity, then he couldn't have healed it, for he could only die for us as one of us.

Jesus took our nature of sinful humanity to redeem us from sin. The film *The Last Temptation of Christ* caused a stir through claims of blasphemy. One key scene that offended many was Jesus on the cross daydreaming about what life would have been like if he had not chosen to die – and he mused, perhaps he would have married Mary Magdalene? Author's licence, and pure conjecture, yes, and not very subtly portrayed, true – but blasphemous? I am not so sure. It certainly challenges us to take seriously the real, actual, visceral humanity of our Lord, about whom the author of the letter to the Hebrews writes, "We do not have a high priest who is unable to sympathize with our weaknesses, but one who in every respect has been tempted as we are, yet without sin" (Hebrews 4:15). Our God is not the abstract unmoved mover of the philosophers, impersonal, unfeeling; no, our God left his dwelling in unapproachable light that we might approach him.

In the apocalyptic movie remake *The Day the Earth Stood Still* Keanu Reeves plays a visitor from outer space who comes to warn humankind of their impending destruction if they don't change their ways. But he is ill-received and ill-treated. So he initiates the destruction of the human race, in order to save the planet. However, as he spends time with a mother and her son, and observes their intimacy, their pain, sorrow, love, and affection, the alien's heart is changed. He decides to have mercy on the world and, at great cost to himself, he averts the coming judgment. It is his experience as a human among humans that moves his actions from judgment to mercy.

Jesus, the eternal divine *logos*,[45] walked among us, in our shoes, as one of us. And although through his divine understanding he understood us better than we understand ourselves, nevertheless his first-hand experience and ill treatment informed him all the more. This not only confirmed that we deserved judgment but also increased, or at least caused him to express more intensely, his mercy for us. Jesus understands me – my pain, shame, weariness, temptations, fears. In love he traversed a way from divinity to humanity, and then through death to life, for me. He became one of us in time so that we might be one with him in eternity. Oh, the wideness of his mercy.

---

45 *Logos* was the Greek term used in John chapter 1 to describe Jesus. It was a term that was taken from Greek philosophy and which described the eternal rationalizing creative principle of the universe.

2. The daughter was dog-bitten

"A woman whose little daughter had an unclean spirit heard of him and came and fell down at his feet" (Mark 7:25),

Though Jesus wanted privacy, somehow the word got out that this miracle-working Messiah was in town. As Mark says in verse 24, he "could not be hidden". Truth will out, light will shine, salt will savour, power will flow, the glory will show, the world will know. God with us cannot be kept secret for long – after all, people know a good thing when they see it. The hungry soon know where to find bread. Word about this man Jesus goes before him. And a desperate mother with a demonized daughter runs to Jesus, for she has heard word that this man has authority to drive out darkness and rout evil spirits.

In the film *The Pink Panther Strikes Back* Inspector Clouseau asks a man who has a dog beside him, "Does your dog bite?" "No," the boy replies. Clouseau bends down: "Good doggy!" Then the dog bites him. "Ouch! I thought you said your dog doesn't bite." The boy replies, "He doesn't. That isn't my dog!"

Just so, the devil is not a tame dog – he is a cornered, rabid dog, snarling and tearing and infecting humanity with its sick saliva. Acting covertly like the coward he is, he sends his emissaries, evil spirits, to enact his architecture of evil. Their purpose is to steal, to kill, and destroy. Satanic squatters, they are invidious invaders who through attrition, affliction, and temptation lead us into sin, superstition, despair, and unbelief.

If we comply with the demonic, they appear to have the ability to manipulate an area of our mind and will, contrary to God's mind and will, and in accordance with Satan's mind and will. Through repeated sin, or being sinned against; through occult involvement, rejecting Christ and embracing false gods; we attract evil spirits who can then gain a foothold of influence in our life. If we persist in complying with evil spirits strongholds of dominance are established, and we become controlled by these spirits in whatever area of our mind and will we have given up.

Like numerous little ropes which bound Gulliver, unbelief, addictions, fears, obsessions, sin, despair, self-destructive behaviour, rebellion toward God, all invite shadows on our spirit. The devil's first tactic is to make you believe he does not exist, so he can work covertly as he ties you in knots. If he is exposed, the devil's second tactic is to tell you that you are powerless to resist, to intimidate and overwhelm you with fear and despair. Both are lies. This woman came because she knew better; she knew her tormented daughter was in the grip of a very present evil, but she also knew Jesus could set the captives free.

Jesus has absolute authority to rout the evil spirits – and they fear his presence and flee at his word. Jesus' whole mercy ministry began with deliverance (Mark 1) which remained central to his ministry and which he commissioned the church to imitate (Mark 16). Jesus healed people when they were sick, forgave sinners, rebuked wrong attitudes, mentored disciples; and often he confronted and expelled demons. He didn't cast demons out of everyone because not everyone has a demon. You cannot deliver what needs discipleship, and you cannot disciple what needs delivering. And so we always need discernment to know what we are dealing with in a presenting issue – is it, for example, a matter for deliverance or for discipleship? But in this case the woman knew it was a demon, and Jesus knew it was a demon.

3. The mother was doggedly determined

"And she begged him to cast the demon out" (Mark 7:26).

The Falklands Islands are 400 miles off the mainland of Argentina and 8,000 miles from Britain. In 1982 President Galtieri thought that the sheer distance meant the British would not be too bothered if he reclaimed them as Argentinian. But he had made a serious miscalculation – he had not reckoned on the tenacity, aggression, and bulldog-like determination of the British prime minister Margaret Thatcher. An enemy had occupied British sovereign territory, and so the "Iron Lady" called the nation to war. British troops crossed the Atlantic in winter and fought a larger, entrenched army to win back the island.

Mark shows us just how determined the Syro-Phoenician woman was to see her child set free from this unclean spirit. The text highlights that, at the very moment she heard Jesus was in town, she came to him and fell down at his feet and begged, beseeched, earnestly entreated him to set the girl free.

Somewhat surprisingly, Jesus responded to this woman's earnest petition by asking whether he should give the children's bread to the dogs. This sharp, racist, profoundly offensive comment sounds utterly uncharacteristic on Jesus' lips. But this is definitely not Jesus' own belief being expressed; he is playing devil's advocate, repeating what his disciples and what any other Jew would be thinking. The rabbis spoke of Israel as God's children and the Gentiles as dogs. Jesus is articulating what the Jews thought, but he does so to expose it as a notion far from what God thinks.

Interestingly, Jesus says deliverance from unclean spirits is bread that belongs to God's children. Does this imply that deliverance is for the children of God first and foremost, and that perhaps even now many Christians need to partake of this bread? When Jesus asks whether he should give the children's bread to dogs, his disciples will have shaken their heads and thought "no". But Jesus knows this woman's faith, and he is about to allow her to speak up to shame the disciples and all who think God racist.

How does this Gentile woman respond to the Jewish thought that God's gifts are only for God's children, the Jews?

Her response reveals great faith, and shames the bigoted. Jesus' apparent put-down does not put her off. "Yes, Lord, but even the dogs eat the crumbs that fall from the table." She is not Jewish, but she has faith and recognizes Jesus as one with spiritual authority, calling him "Lord". She is not defensive, she takes no offence, and does not consider herself more highly than she ought. She is humble and does not plead on the basis of any merit she might muster. No, she is willing to be thought a dog – and that gives her an image through which to express her faith: "Even the dogs eat the scraps." She will settle for scraps from the Saviour.

Her persistence pays off. Blessed are the meek, for they shall inherit the kingdom of heaven. This woman does not presume on Christ, but she's not too proud to plead with Christ. She does not treat Jesus like a utility but with reverence and respect. She honours him, and he honours her. She humbles herself under his mighty hand, and he exalts her. Without faith it is impossible to please God, but this woman has faith by the bucketload, and God loves to respond to faith's perseverance and petitioning.

Ask and you will receive, seek and you will find, knock and the door will be opened to you. Jacob would not let go of God until God blessed him – and he was blessed. Bartimaeus would not stop screaming until Jesus heard, heeded, and healed him. How sad that the British are tenacious in everything except their pursuit of God! A Frenchwoman once told me that the reason Wellington won at Waterloo was because the British would not give in, whereas the French got bored. What freedom we would enjoy, what fruit we would see, what souls we would save, if only we exhibited the same dogged spirit for God that this woman demonstrated.

4. The demon was doggone

"'For this statement you may go your way; the demon has left your daughter.' And she went home and found the child lying in bed and the demon gone" (Mark 7:29–30).

Jesus said: "If the Son sets you free, you will be free indeed" (John 8:36). And he set this tormented girl free – indeed! Jesus does not reluctantly acquiesce to her debating skills; no, he willingly responds to her faith-filled persistence. Jesus never met a demon he liked, nor a demon he couldn't handle. This is the reason the Son of Man appeared – "to destroy the works of the evil one". Jesus once asked: "When the Son of Man comes, will he find faith on earth?" (Luke 18:8). He found too little of it in Israel, and he certainly did not find it with the Pharisees, Sadducees and Jewish authorities. But he found faith with a pagan Syro-Phoenician woman and her faith opened his heart and hand, and from a distance he worked deliverance. What mercy, what power.

I once bought an old Bible in a second-hand bookshop. What attracted me to it was the handwritten inscription. The owner had written at the top the date July 1892, then the words: "I will run the way of thy commandments when thou hast set my heart at liberty. For the Lord your God is gracious and will not turn away his face from you if ye return unto him". These reveal the man's intent to seek God and find freedom.

Underneath this, in different ink, he writes again two months later. These were two months known only to him, his God, the angels and the demons; two months of turning, running, seeking, and obeying the Lord; two months of prayer, petitioning and pleading with Christ. For now he writes triumphantly: "At last, I know the truth. Free, free."

Jesus is a merciful God who came to set the captives free.

Chapter 12
Salt of the Earth

But these few are the salt of the earth; without them, human life would become a stagnant pool. Not only is it they who introduce good things which did not before exist, it is they who keep the life in those which already existed.[46]
John Stuart Mill

Lately, salt has been getting a bad press: we are told that our diet contains too much of it, especially in ready-made microwave or tinned foods, and that too much salt has serious detrimental effects to our health, like cholesterol levels, blood pressure, and heart disease.

But we do well to remember that salt is essential for life.[47] Against the flow of popular opinion Dr Michael Alderman, Chairman of Epidemiology at Albert Einstein School of Medicine in New York, says America's health is poor because of too little salt: "The lower the sodium the worse off you are." Consider the following facts:

- Sea salt stabilizes irregular heartbeats
- Sea salt is vital to enable brain and body cells to pass and process information

---

46 *On Liberty*, Chapter 3, Section 11, p. 124.
47 http://shawn-king.com/blog/wellnesscoach/1102/16-important-functions-of-real-sea-salt/

- Sea salt is vital for absorption of food particles through the intestines
- Sea salt is vital for clearing lungs of mucous plugs in cystic fibrosis and asthma
- Sea salt is a strong natural antihistamine
- Sea salt is vital for the prevention of muscle cramps
- Sea salt is vital to making the structure of bones firm
- Sea salt is a natural hypnotic, vital for sleep regulation
- Sea salt on the tongue will stop persistent dry coughs
- Sea salt is vital for the prevention of gout and arthritis
- Sea salt is vital for maintaining libido
- Sea salt is vital for preventing varicose veins and spider veins
- Sea salt is vital for reducing a double chin – lack of salt causes glands to secrete more fluid to break up food that leaks into jowls.

It is an inescapable fact that salt is essential to physical well-being and, metaphorically, to our spiritual well-being. Jesus said, "You are the salt of the earth!" What did he mean?

Salt was a precious commodity in the ancient world. The Greeks said that salt was *divine*, the purest of all things. The Romans prized it, saying *"Nil utilis sole et sale"* – "Nothing is as valuable as sun and salt." It was essential to health in the hot Middle East, where sweating evacuated the body of natural salts and brought severe medical conditions, as noted in our list above. Roman soldiers were often paid wages in salt. Indeed our word salary comes from the Latin *salarium*, which referred to salt pay.

As well as keeping good health, salt was used to "savour the pot", to improve the flavour of food, and to "stop the rot" – being one of the very first antibiotics applied to heal infected wounds. In the many centuries before refrigerators, salt was rubbed into meat and fish to prevent bacteria and flies from ruining meat – unsalted meat in a hot climate would be running in maggots within a day, whereas salted meat could last weeks, even months! The ancient Persian, Chinese, and Romans used salt as manure, a natural fertilizer! What an amazing resource – insecticide, germicide, fertilizer. It even had a mystical conception, and Romans scattered it on the site where a crime had been committed, as if to exorcize away the evil; the Roman church has long used "blessed salt" to be sprinkled in places and on people for exorcism and healing.

Biblically, we see salt had an important religious use: Jewish priests added it to most offerings (Leviticus 2:13; Numbers 18:19; Ezra 6:9) and it was an essential component in incense (Exodus 30:35). Salt was also used as a symbol of covenant – to eat salt with someone was an act of loyalty, peace, and commitment (Ezra 4:14; Mark 9:50) and is still used in this way today in Arab cultures, cementing friendship and agreements.

Did Jesus have all these conceptions of salt in mind when he used it as a metaphor describing his disciples (Matthew 5:13)? Certainly many of them – he understood the church as God's special gift to the world, here to improve the flavour of the earth; holding back the defiling rot of sin; spiritually facilitating earth's offering as sacrifice to God (Romans 15:16); interceding for the needs of the world like incense before God; and we are a symbol before God and his world of the covenant of salvation and the commitment God has made to the world in Christ.

Let us not miss the remarkable context of all this: in the preceding verses (Matthew 5:10–12) Jesus has said the world will reject the church and persecute her. But rather than respond in kind Christ's followers are to enter deep into the world so that, by being who she is, she transforms it. Jesus actually says: "You, you are the salt of the earth" – there is an emphasis in the Greek text where the pronoun "you" is added to enforce the verb "you are". Jesus is quite clear: you, *yes, you* are the salt. Not the Torah, not the Temple, not the religious leaders, but you, the disciples of Jesus.

You are the salt – present tense – not "you will be, may be, could be," but you are, here and now! Our vocation is to be salt, our location is here on earth. To speak of "salting the earth" shows God's yes and his no to it. God's yes, because he has not given up on it, and desires to transform it. God's no, because the world is not as it should be, and needs protecting, preserving, purifying, and perfecting.

To speak of "the earth" shows Christ's remarkable confidence in what transformation can be achieved. Initially this came through a few humble, unsophisticated, uneducated Galileans, but their influence reached throughout the course of history and to the uttermost ends of the earth. This shows God's global perspective: he is not some parochial divine, no mere tribal god for a small handful of elect Jews. The God who created the whole earth wants to be related to the earth.

To speak of "the earth" shows that God is not simply interested in saving souls – Jesus does not speak of salting humankind or the *kosmos* (the world). His term *ge* means creation – the earth and all that is upon it. Here are hints of the mandate given to Adam to care and steward creation. Being the salt of the earth involves an ecological vocation.

1. To be the salt of the earth we must be present to it

There is a biblical thread that says we are "citizens in heaven", pilgrims passing briefly through earth. But many in the monastic and pietistic or dispensational traditions have gone further and developed an unbiblical dualism which essentially results in considering anything spiritual as good, while matter does not matter. As the saying rightly reminds us, we can become so heavenly minded as to be of no earthly use. Salt of the earth must be in the earth to salt it.

The 1994 World Cup Football celebrations were initiated in a French stadium where a girl read a poem enthralling billions of viewers in which she said: "Take us to a better place." Many followers of Jesus have just such an escapist mindset. But Jesus says to us, "I'm sending you into this earth as salt to make *it* a better place." We are to be world-affirming and world-transforming. Dietrich Bonhoeffer spoke of Jesus as the "man for others", the one who lived his life and gave his life for others. Bonhoeffer called us to a vision where Jesus is at the centre of our lives, we are at the centre of the church, and the church is at the centre of the world. Regrettably, often the church has operated in a centripetal rather than centrifugal manner, with all its movement going inward to the centre, as everything is sucked into church activity. But if we are to be salt of the earth, church activity must spiral in an outward direction away from the centre.

We are to be present in a prophetic, "salty" lifestyle. The Word became flesh and dwelt among us, but sadly the church has often withdrawn into religious cliques. Good for nothing. Martin Luther said, "Salt is not salt for itself." It serves its purpose not in a jar but in a meal. Salt that sits just a centimetre from the food is worthless. We don't expect the food to place itself in the salt-cellar, but the salt is placed in the food. So why do we expect people to come to church? We the church should go to the world.

I recall hearing how one mission-minded "Fresh Expression" church encouraged all its members, as part of their discipleship, to be regular members of nightclubs, poetry clubs, sports clubs... intentionally there as salt. Salt-glaze pottery produces wonderful clay pots when fired in the oven. The unique finish is effected by a handful of salt thrown into the kiln, which vaporizes and gives the pot its wonderful glossy coat. Christ wants us to be in the kiln of life, putting a godly shine on it all as our influence spreads. We need politicians, law-makers, economists, educationalists, artists, industrialists, all salted by Christ and the gospel, bringing God's kingdom here on earth as it is in heaven.

2. We are to be salty through our prayers for the earth

Consider the biblical use of salt in incense. We can salt the earth through prayer-walking through the streets, led by the Spirit to intercede for the needs we see and sense around us. We can sit down for set prayers at 6:00 and 10:00 while watching the news, being led and bled in prayer for our hurting world. In our family, work place, schools, colleges, down our street, our regular journeys – let us be salting through praying. We can take risks, be salty and ask people, "Is there something I can pray for to bless you?" Go on, try it – you will be amazed how people respond favourably and open up to you.

The first petition Jesus taught his disciples to pray was, "Your kingdom come, your will be done, on earth as it is in heaven" (Matthew 6:10). Often that is the last on our list. Prayer is a work of salting the earth, transforming the earth, invoking God's rule on the earth. It is a work of justice and mercy.

3. We are to be salty through presenting Christ

We ought always to be seeking to bring Jesus' name, work, teaching, and spirit into our conversation and activities. Christ is the transformative agent in us that changes things. Salt is Christ's holy love, in us, in the world, in action.

However, Catholic priest and author, Brennan Manning, says that something has gone very wrong in our communication of the gospel of Jesus when the latest perfume is called *Grace*. When the world can take an eternity-changing, God-impacting word and reduce its use to that of a spray-on perfume, we have devalued our message and witness. We have failed to convey through word and deed how amazing grace really is. We need to look for new ways and new words to present the unchanging gospel.

Canon Robin Gamble, former Missioner at Manchester Cathedral, heard comedienne Jo Brand on the radio commenting that all clergy looked depressed. He rather agreed and decided to write to her, inviting her to address 400 Manchester clergy and their spouses. On the letter-headed paper from the cathedral was his formal title "Canon Evangelist Robin Gamble". When Ms Brand replied, in all seriousness, she wrote, "I note your title, Canon Evangelist. I assume you are not of the Anglican persuasion." Based on her experience she did not believe that the Church of England did evangelism! She did not accept the invitation.

The gospel of Jesus Christ is the hope of the world, but people need to hear it from us, and see its benefit in us; they need to encounter Christ in the gospel, not our take on the gospel, our particular doctrinal emphasis. I read of some zealous evangelists, reported in *The Times* newspaper, shouting to folk on a train, "Don't you know you will all rot in hell!" That is not good news. That does not convey the glory of grace. That does not present Jesus in a winsome way. And that is not salty.

4. We are to be salty through our prophetic lifestyle

There is an often quoted saying credited to St Francis: "Preach the gospel, use words if you have to." The gospel always involves words – it needs to be preached to all creation as Jesus commanded (Mark 16:15). However, it often needs to be seen to be believed. People have to see the work the salt has done in our lives before they will welcome it in theirs. When American journalist Henry Stanley discovered David Livingstone in Central Africa, he spent four months with the doctor. Later he wrote:

> *In 1871, I went to search for him as prejudiced as the biggest atheist in London. To a reporter and correspondent, such as I, who had only to deal with wars, mass meetings, and political gatherings; sentimental matters were entirely out of my province. But there came for me a long time for reflection. I was out there away from a worldly world. I saw this solitary old man there, and asked myself, "How on earth does he stop here – is he cracked or what? What is it that inspires him?" For months after we met I simply found myself listening to him, wondering at the old man carrying out all that was said in the Bible… But little by little… my sympathy was aroused; seeing his piety, his gentleness, his zeal, his earnestness… I was converted by him although he had not tried to do it. It was not Livingstone's preaching which converted me. It was Livingstone's living![48]*

Have we ever drawn people to Christ by being ourselves? Jesus said they'll know you're Christians by your love – it is love for one another and our fellow humanity that is to be a defining feature of our saltiness.

As well as love, salt is defined by its purity. Indeed, it cannot purify or function as a transforming agent if it is impure itself. There was uproar recently when a George Barna report, having compared and contrasted the moral behaviour of evangelicals with non-churched people, concluded, "We rarely find substantial

---

48 Joseph S. Exell, *The Biblical Illustrator.*

differences." Barna Project Director Meg Flammang said: "We would love to be able to report that Christians are living very distinct lives and impacting the community, but … in the area of divorce rates they continue to be the same."[49]

This prophetic salty lifestyle is radical and servant-hearted. While the world has a preference for success and power, we follow Jesus who emptied himself and took the form of a slave. Jesus inverts the world's values; he is downwardly mobile, moving toward the broken, rejected, and outcast – the ragamuffins, the lepers, and the loose women. Yet although Jesus was downwardly mobile, when he moved into an area it went upmarket, because he transformed lives. And his salty disciples are to do likewise.

Hannah More was the salt of the earth and sought to give free education to the illiterate poor. William Wilberforce was the salt of the earth and fought to free the oppressed slave. The Earl of Shaftesbury was the salt of the earth and fought in the courts to ban child labour. Catherine Booth was the salt of the earth and rescued girls from dark alleys and prostitution. Dr Barnardo was the salt of the earth and sought to give unwanted orphans a family and a home. Paul Brand was the salt of the earth and gave new limbs and new lives to lepers in India. Oxfam, Tearfund, the Red Cross, World Vision, Viva Network, Operation International – all Christian organizations, salt of the earth, making the world a better place in Christ's name.

The apostle Peter said the Gentiles should see our good deeds and glorify God (1 Peter 2:12). Have you ever known of a non-Christian praising God for the good they have seen in you or gained from you? Graham Mytton, former head of BBC World Service audience relations, once declared, "AIDS offers the greatest chance for the church to show its true colours." Confronted by overwhelming tragedy, we can make a difference, if we want and if we will. Yes, the church has often got it wrong, she has

49 http://www.religioustolerance.org/chr_dira.htm

failed God and the world. Much that has been done in her name has been wicked – wars fought, cultures shredded, injustices legitimated. She has baptized nations' will to power. But on a good day, she has been great. When she has obeyed her master's great commission, when she has proclaimed the gospel, when she has been present to the world, when she has lived prophetically, when she has been the salt of the earth, then she has been glorious. Miranda in Shakespeare's *The Tempest* says, "O brave new world that has such people in it."[50] If Christ is in us, and if we are in the world, then what a brave and beautiful world we will create.

5. Jesus warns of salt at fault

"If salt has lost its taste … It is no longer good for anything except to be thrown out and trampled under people's feet" (Matthew 5:13). On first impressions, this is a strange saying, as salt is one of the most stable of elements. But it can be diluted by water or by the additions of other elements. So the Roman scholar Pliny wrote: "Salt mixed with impurities becomes useless." Jesus is saying that we who are called to be salt and transform our environment may fail our vocation by being transformed by it.

This was certainly the history of Israel. Called out to be God's people as a witness and influence to the nations, instead they "mixed with the nations and learned to do as they did. They served their idols" (Psalm 106:35–36). The church is often simply living below par, living beneath her birthright, the dowdy rather than beautiful bride of Christ. I think large parts of the church have lost confidence. We have lost sight of God, lost the gospel, lost the leaven of heaven… lost the Saviour's salt. Oh, how we need the church to be salted so it can salt society.

When Hitler came to power, he did it with the backing and votes of the majority of Christians – Lutheran and Catholic. The

---

50 *The Tempest*, Act 5, Scene 1.

party of politicized Christians called "The German Christians" actually lauded Hitler in messianic terms, believing his rhetoric to create the Third Reich (the third millennium reign of God on earth). They rejoiced when a Nazi bishop was appointed to Hitler's cabinet and opened rallies with prayers. Many of their top theologians went to work justifying Nazism, condemning Jews, presenting an Aryan Gentile Jesus. The salt had lost its saltiness and actually became poison.

The church has often sold out to the world in less dramatic but no less disastrous ways. Rather than be prophetic, manifesting justice and mercy, she has accommodated to the world's values and views. The nineteenth-century Danish philosopher Søren Kierkegaard recorded how:

> *In the splendid cathedral, the high, well-born, highly honoured, and worthy Geheime-General-Ober-Hof-Preacher, the chosen darling of the important people, steps before a select circle of the select, and movingly sermonizes on a text chosen by himself, namely, "God has chosen the lowly and despised of the earth" – and no one laughs.*[51]

Kierkegaard saw the great gulf of inconsistency between what the church practised and what she preached.

When Jesus says that if it loses its saltiness it is fit to be thrown out and trampled on, he may just be offering us a second chance. There was a custom in ancient Judaism where, if a person had left or been rejected by the synagogue in shame and sin, they could if repentant be readmitted by enacting a strange rite. They lay at the door of the synagogue while the worshippers walked over them as they entered and left. Having humbled themselves and been walked over, they were readmitted to fellowship. Perhaps Jesus is saying that even if we have failed to live for Christ, to be

---

51 Quoted in Joakim Garff, *Søren Kierkegaard*, p. 774.

justice and mercy, we can be made salty again, though only by contrition, humility, and repentance.

Like those traditional crisps that have a small blue salt sachet inside the bag, which you have to tear open to sprinkle the salt, the church in the world needs to be taken out, torn open and poured back in, to flavour it with justice and mercy.

The church grew by being salty

Sociologist and historian of religion, Rodney Stark, has written a powerful book called *The Rise of Christianity*. His basic thesis is that the church advanced not because of her impressive apologetic defence, or persuasive preaching, but primarily because of her public acts of grace and mercy which endeared the suffering society to her. When commenting on how Christianity was good news for "women", Stark observed:

> *Christian women had tremendous advantages compared to the woman next door, who was like them in every way except that she was a pagan. First, when did you get married? Most pagan girls were married off around age 11, before puberty, and they had nothing to say about it, and they got married to some 35-year-old guy. Christian women had plenty of say in the matter and tended to marry around age 18. Abortion was a huge killer of women in this period, but Christian women were spared that. And infanticide – pagans killed little girls left and right. We've unearthed sewers clogged with the bones of newborn girls. But Christians prohibited this. Consequently, the sex ratio changed and Christians didn't have the enormous shortage of women that plagued the rest of the empire.*[52]

---

52 http://www.catholiceducation.org/articles/history/world/wh0140.htm

Reflecting further on Stark's thesis, theologian Dr Stephen Backhouse recently wrote to me:

> *In 165 a plague swept through the mighty Roman Empire, wiping out one in three of the population. It happened again in 251 when 5,000 people per day were dying in the city of Rome alone. Those infected were abandoned by their families to die in the streets. The government was helpless and the Emperor himself succumbed to the plague. Pagan priests fled their temples where people had flocked for comfort and explanation. People were too weak to help themselves. If the smallpox did not kill you, hunger, thirst and loneliness would. The effect on wider society was catastrophic. Yet following the plagues the good reputation of Christianity was confirmed, and its population grew exponentially. Why is this? Christians did not come armed with intellectual answers to the problem of evil. They did not enjoy a supernatural ability to avoid pain and suffering. What they did have was water and food and their presence. In short, if you knew a Christian you were statistically more likely to survive, and if you survived it was the church that offered you the most loving, stable and social environment. It was not clever apologetics, strategic political organisation or the witness of martyrdom which converted an Empire, so much as it was the simple conviction of normal women and men that what they did for the least of their neighbours they did it for Christ.*

Throughout history Christians really have been the salt of the earth, while the Crusades and Inquisitions and power-plays and compromises also show that often they have often lost their saltiness. How are we doing today?

Chapter 13

Restoring the Splendour

*Men who are occupied in the restoration of health to
other men, by the joint exertion of skill and humanity,
are above all the great of the earth. They even partake
of divinity, since to preserve and renew is almost as
noble as to create.*[53]
Voltaire

God is in the creation and restoration business.

Jesus restored sight to the man born blind.

Jesus restored life to the dead boy and a son to his
grieving mother.

Jesus restored dignity to the woman caught in adultery.

Jesus restored sanity to the Gadarene demonic.

Jesus restored fallen humankind to their Father God.

The Old Testament prophet Nahum declared these words: "The
Lord will restore the splendour of Jacob like the splendour
of Israel, though destroyers have laid them waste and have
ruined their vines" (Nahum 2:2 NIV). This echoed round the
forlorn exiled Jewish community, rousing hope. These words
– restore, splendour, laid waste (literally, "emptied out") –
convey something essential to what God often sees of the human
condition, and what God always wants to do and bring about for

---

53 Francois Marie Arouet de Voltaire, *Philosophical Dictionary*, first published
in 1764.

us. The Spirit of God is ever seeking to restore the emptiness and ruin of the human condition and to fill it with splendour.

Emptied out

The Hebrew is *baqaq*, an onomatopoeic word, which sounds like the word used for the gurgling of a flask as its contents are poured out. Israel has been drained, laid waste by her enemy Assyria who has plundered and ransacked. This emptiness is a consequence of both Israel's sin against God, which has pulled down her walls of protection and made her vulnerable, and of her being sinned against by the cruel martial Assyria. Emptiness is the experience of all who have turned their backs on God, or never turned their faces to him. Helen Keller, the American social activist who was blind and deaf from infancy yet sought after God, wrote:

> *Once I knew only darkness and stillness... my life was without past or future... but a little word from the fingers of another fell into my hand that clutched at emptiness, and my heart leaped to the rapture of living.*

Restore

God says he is about to restore Israel's splendour. What has been stolen will be replaced: the vines – a common symbol of Israel – will again bear grapes and produce new wine. The message of the prophets often involved the twins rebuke and restoration: rebuke of the sin that has brought them into ruin, and promise of restoration if they will repent. The prophets spoke grace and judgment, judgment and grace. God is a restoring God – the dry bones will live again (Ezekiel), God will repay you for the years the locust have eaten (Joel), the glory of the latter temple will be greater than the former (Habakkuk) the adulterous wife will be welcomed back and loved by her husband (Hosea).

Art critic and designer, John Ruskin, said:

> *It is impossible, as impossible as to raise the dead, to restore anything that has ever been great or beautiful in architecture. That which I have insisted upon as the life of the whole, that spirit which is given only by the hand and eye of the workman, can never be recalled.*[54]

Is restoration impossible? Not so. God the eternal architect is still with us, his initial plans and designs remain; he restored Israel to the land from slavery, and the ruined temple to its former glory. Jesus restored sight to the blind, baby-smooth skin to the leper, hope to the despairing, dignity to the adulteress, life to the dead. What man ruins, God can restore.

Splendour

The Hebrew is *gaon* from a root meaning "pride, rising, exalting, height". In the modern Hebrew language it refers to "genius rabbis", but biblically it conveyed the sense of "majesty, honour, excellence, splendour". Israel is in ruins, but God sees that she will rise again, restored and magnificent. A few years ago on the BBC TV programme *The Antiques Roadshow*, a man brought along a tired old painting. While going fishing, he had found it thrown away on the side of the road next to a rubbish dump, and subsequently he kept it for years in an attic along with old magazines and household junk. The original owners subsequently came forward and made a claim on it, proving their ownership, and arguing it had been stolen decades earlier. It turned out to be an original watercolour by the famed American impressionist

---

54 John Ruskin, *The Lamp of Memory*, Sections 18–20.

Winslow Homer. It was taken to the art restorers and all the layers of accumulated dirt and damage were taken off. The paint damage was replaced and the original vibrant colours brought out. Its estimated value is now in excess of $250,000. Something beautiful, stolen, ruined and lost... now found and restored.

God is restoring Israel to the land

Nahum says that God is restoring Jacob and Israel. He is not simply repeating himself by using the two names here. Since Solomon's death the tribes of Israel have been painfully divided – Judah in the south and Israel in the north. But here Nahum's reference to Israel refers to the southern kingdom, while "Jacob" is his term for the north. This promise to restore Israel and Jacob goes beyond the immediate prophetic context of removing the enemy Assyria and looks toward the reuniting of these families in conflict. That which God promised God delivered, albeit not immediately. God's covenant with Israel allowed them to live in the land on the condition that they remained faithful to the Lord. Because of their sin and rebellion the covenant was broken, and this resulted in their repeated invasion and ultimate exile under the Assyrians, followed by the Babylonians, and finally the Romans.

Restoring the splendour of Israel has always been God's heart. But first Israel as a nation was scattered to the four winds, after the destruction of Jerusalem in AD 70. There was a brief but forlorn uprising in the Jewish wars of 132–35, but for nearly 2,000 years she wandered as a vagrant throughout the world, like an unwelcome, uninvited guest. Most Christian nations used or abused the Jews (only the Dutch Protestants and Puritans under Cromwell welcomed them). Pogroms and persecutions became Israel's daily diet, culminating in the horrors of Nazi Germany's holocaust which sought to eradicate her once and for all, as if they might remove every trace of Israel's DNA from the human race and thwart God's declared promise to restore her to the land before his return there. But throughout those wilderness years, God never forgot the apple of his eye, his first covenant people. He has remained faithful even if they have not. He promised through the prophets: "I will restore the fortunes of my people Israel, and they shall rebuild the ruined cities and inhabit them" (Amos 9:14); "Then I will gather the remnant of my flock out of all the countries where I have driven them, and I will bring them back to their fold, and they shall be fruitful and multiply" (Jeremiah 23:3). Though slow in fulfilment, its time would come.

We must be careful not to over-spiritualize these prophetic promises and make them spiritual metaphors for the restoration of souls becoming Christians. That would be to eviscerate them of the very hope they offered – and it would be to remove the plain meaning and import an alien one, a million miles from the minds of the prophets. The promise in the prophecies is of a restoration of Jews, from all tribes, to the land once called Israel.

This expectation and longing for a restoring of Israel is voiced by the disciples after the resurrection when they asked Jesus, "Lord, will you at this time restore the kingdom to Israel?" (Acts 1:6). Significantly, Jesus did not say, "You have it wrong, guys, there will be no restoration of Israel, it's now a matter of a spiritual global kingdom from here on in." He simply stated, "It is not for you to know times or seasons the Father has fixed by his own authority" (Acts 1:7). Here Jesus was surely saying that there would come a time and date for the restoration of the kingdom of Israel – a time when Israel would be its own kingdom, under its own rule, and not under the rule of Babylonians, Assyrians, Romans, or anyone else. The Father has set the time and date by his authority. It will not be established by the whim or will of human authority.

For 1,700 years those remaining in Israel, ancestors of those who returned from Babylon under Ezra and Nehemiah – Judahites and Benjaminites – were also banished from the land. And although the other ten tribes of the northern kingdom had already been scattered to the four winds, intermingled and intermarried, miraculously God preserved his people in exile. Many never forget where they came from or who they came from – Abraham, Isaac, and Jacob. It is nothing short of a miracle that Israel survived as a distinct racial group, especially as she had no homeland borders to guard her and define her. But the Abrahamic DNA remained intact and distinct – the memory of Jewish ancestry was not lost. Where now are the other distinct races such as the Jebusites, Hittites, and Amalekites? All of their DNA has dissipated into larger generic people groups. But the Jewish people, the descendants of Abraham, Isaac, and Jacob are still very much with us.

The Father has set the time and date by his authority for Israel's restoration. And, it seems to me at least, as well as to others within the Christian community, that this restoration was initiated in 1948. The formation of the State of Israel was no mere accident of history, not by the decree of the League of Nations, but as God's prophetic fulfilment. This was no mere momentary global show of conscience and compassion for a persecuted people in the wake of Auschwitz and Belsen. God had promised through Nahum and his prophets to remove Jacob and Israel's emptiness, to restore her to the land and to her former splendour. And then 2,500 years after Nahum's prophecy, 1,800 years after her banishment to the four winds, she was re-established as a nation state in the land sworn to her ancestors – all in a day. And large tracts of unpopulated, uninhabitable, barren, malaria-filled swampland have become one of the most yield-productive agricultures in the world

Now, do not misunderstand me. I am not an uncritical Zionist. I would not put God's name to much of Israel's military and social policy. I do not believe she is righteous, "right with God", nor do I believe her Jewishness justifies her when she acts without justice and mercy. The politics of Israel are complex, but justice is objective – and she must live righteously in the land if she is to remain in the land. David must not become Goliath. Israel is largely a secular state; ironically the most devout Jews in the land do not believe it was God who restored her there, believing 1948 to have been a phantom pregnancy. Christian Zionists must recognize the nation state of Israel is secular in its foundation and its population largely reject the God of Israel. God has restored Israel to the land, but Israel have not yet been restored to the Lord. Nevertheless, God is faithful to his word, and he fulfils his purposes. The promise "I have loved Jacob" (Malachi 1:2) has not been revoked. God desires and has decreed that all Israel will be saved, I anticipate that, having returned to the land, Israel will turn to the Lord. Meanwhile, as Israel is restored to the land and as she restores the land, she must be very careful to honour the alien in her midst, those former residents who are now refugees. If she fails to show justice and mercy, she will incur not only God's wrath but also the raging of the nations.

We have seen a strange shift in sixty years since the Holocaust, from an almost global cry for justice and mercy for the Jews, a justice and mercy that would establish a homeland for them, to the cry for the Palestinians, the 700,000-plus displaced from their homeland as Israel established theirs. That number has grown to seven million, but their cry for justice and mercy has largely been refused by their Arab neighbours who won't integrate the Palestinians into their lands, though they are happy to use them as a rod to beat Israel. The Palestinians have repeatedly rejected Israel's terms for peace as "not enough", most notably Yasser Arafat's rejection of Ehud Barak's offer at Camp David in 2000[55] which would have given them 90 per cent

---

55 http://articles.cnn.com/2011-05-24/world/israel.1967_1_netanya-israeli-forces-syria-and-jordan/2?_s=PM:WORLD

of the land they were asking for. We must pray that both the Jew and Palestinian may sit in peace, each under his own olive tree; that both may experience justice and mercy.

God is restoring creation as the panoply of his glory

Interestingly the Hebrew word *gaon* "splendour" is often used in conjunction with creation, as in lush thickets or vibrant vegetation. The prophecy about the renewing of the vines is not simply a metaphor about Israel's restoration, or of living peaceably and prospering, able to grow crops, to harvest and enjoy their fruit. The hearers of this "word" would have immediately visualized restoration of "splendour" in terms of Jordan's rich pasture land and lush forests (Isaiah 10:18).

One repeated theme seen in the prophets is that the land itself suffers when the people suffer under judgment for covenant infidelity. This is true beyond the borders of Israel. Sin always has consequences on our environment not just on our souls. God created the world and declared it was good. He appointed Adam as a steward, a gardener in paradise. And the mandate passes to all Adam's heirs. But tragically humankind has often failed miserably in her responsibility to husband the earth. The creation that manifests divine power and glory is now deeply scarred and bears the wounds inflicted by humankind. Let me suggest some possible reasons for this:

1. The influence of Greek Platonic dualism. This was disastrous for creation ethics because of its emphasis on the spiritual over the physical. The material is regarded as an almost demonic distant devolution from the divine. This sadly influenced the church, which puts its theological weight behind spiritual

matters (the soul and spirit), despising the physical (sex was out, fasting in).

2. The influence of the Enlightenment. This placed too great an emphasis on the individual as thinking subject, or the ultimate evolved creature, rather than on their co-dependent place in their eco-system.

3. The influence of materialism, which has sought short-term quick profits, utilizing the earth's resources today at the sake of the next generation tomorrow.

4. The influence of sheer ignorance. We are only now really beginning to understand the impact of our human actions on the delicate symbiotic eco-systems God has created. And so we find ourselves in this world that God created beautiful, to reveal his splendour and majesty, on the brink of disaster. Unsustainable population increase, damaging crop science, poisonous household waste, Amazon forest land-grabbing, carbon emissions, ozone layer holes, polar ice caps melting, sea levels rising, dramatic climate changes, numerous endangered species, tsunami waves... we are on the brink of an ecological crisis as disastrous as a thermo-nuclear exchange. Shockingly, as long ago as 1966, the American historian-scientist Dr Lynn White said: "Christianity is to blame for the ecological crisis that threatens – Christianity is the most anthropocentric, nature-exploiting religion the world has ever seen."[56] Has "saving souls" for heaven resulted in disregard for this habitation?

Scripture says that when Christ returns he will create new heavens and a new earth, destroying what exists by fire (2 Peter 3:10–13).

56 Lynn White, Jr, "The Historical Roots of Our Ecological Crisis" published in *Science*, Vol. 155, pp. 1203–1207, and responded to in http://www.btinternet.com/~j.p.richardson/lynnwhite.html

Some traditions within the church have suggested that if it's all going up in fire, if it's all going to be destroyed and a new one created in its place, then we need not bother with what we have here and now. But the mandate given to Adam, contained within the very first command God uttered to us, was that we husband and steward the creation. I do not believe this mandate has been revoked. And even while creation groans, awaiting the day of its redemption and liberation, we obey God's command and partner with God's Spirit to restore the splendour of creation.

Christ is restoring his bride to her destiny

Twice in the Song of Songs (6:4, 10) the Beloved describes his bride as "awesome as an army with banners" – hardly a typical metaphor a groom uses of his bride! However, if we follow the long Jewish and Christian tradition in interpreting this letter as a celebration of the intimacy between the Messiah and his church, then it makes more sense. Christ celebrates his bride as an army. But is she an awesome army with banners? In C. S. Lewis's meditation *The Screwtape Letters* the demon Screwtape is training a junior demon in sabotaging God's purposes. He says:

> *One of our greatest allies [in opposing the work of Christ] is the church itself. Don't misunderstand me, I do not mean the church as we see her, spread through all time and space, rooted in eternity, terrible as an army with banners. That is, I confess, a spectacle which makes our boldest tempters uneasy – but fortunately it is quite invisible.*[57]

The demon Screwtape understands the church's destiny to be an awesome army in advancing God's kingdom, and he has witnessed this in the eternal mystical body of the church. But he

---

57 C. S. Lewis, *The Screwtape Letters*, Letter 2, p. 12.

is reassured by the fact that the church in her current presentation does not come close to being a terrifying foe.

Many New Testament epistles are written in an attempt to restore the glory and majesty to the church. Invariably the authors challenge the church that has fallen away from following Christ faithfully and into sin or doctrinal error. In Revelation six out of the seven churches Jesus addresses have fallen from their splendour and need to be restored. The church is challenged to hold on to the truth, to repent, to remember, to do as she did before. And any cursory glance at church history reveals that God is constantly seeking to restore a crooked church to the plumb line of the kingdom of God and the gospel of Jesus.

Are we an army with banners or an army in tatters? Do we make demons tremble or smile? I think the church today in the West is more often like the British Expeditionary Force at Dunkirk than a victorious and glorious army leading captives in its triumphant procession. Søren Kierkegaard said, "It would be utterly impossible for the first Christians to recognize Christianity in its current distortion."[58]

God is always restoring the splendour of his church. At any moment he is wanting to work on one of the three core areas of her life: *doctrinal* (the core tenets of her faith); *experiential* (her knowledge of the love, power, and holiness of God) and *practical* (her mission, her ethics, her cultural engagement). In the sixteenth and seventeenth centuries God was restoring her doctrinally, especially with regard to our justification by faith and the priesthood of all believers. In the seventeenth and eighteenth centuries God was restoring us practically, in terms of global mission, when numerous missions were established. In the late nineteenth and twentieth centuries God has been restoring the church experientially, in our understanding of holiness and the Spirit-filled life.

---

58 Quoted in *Provocations*, compiled by Charles Moore, p. 205.

As we advance into the twenty-first century, I believe the Lord is restoring the splendour of the church to her first love of Christ; restoring the church in her understanding of the end time purposes for Israel – both people and place; restoring the church in her holiness as she washes her robes; restoring the church in her doctrine especially relating to the nature of the kingdom and the content of the gospel; restoring the church in her worship of God in intimacy, Spirit and truth; restoring the church in her prime commitment to engagement in social justice. Jesus wants to return to a bride prepared and a world evangelized. And that day of his return is nearer than when we began.

Christ is restoring people to the glory of his image

Romans 1:23 states that the unrighteous "exchanged the glory of the immortal God for images resembling mortal man and birds and animals" and 3:23 confirms that "all have sinned and fall short of the glory of God".

But that is not the whole story, and it certainly isn't the good news – "And we all, with unveiled face, beholding the glory of the Lord, are being transformed into the same image from one degree of glory to another" (2 Corinthians 3:18).

When our forefather Adam rebelled, he forfeited the divine glory. This was not simply the glory of knowing the presence of God; the glory of the image of God in him was marred. Ever since, humankind has not been what God intended. The glory had departed, and *Ichabod* (see 1 Samuel 4) was written over us.

But the cross of Christ is the forgiveness of sins, the Spirit of Christ is the restoration of our status as divine sons in his image – and this is glorious splendour. The second-century Church Father Irenaeus said, "The glory of God is man fully alive." Just as in

156

The Narnia Chronicles Aslan breathed on those who had become frozen statues through the curse of the white witch, bringing them back to life, so Christ breathes his Spirit on us and brings us back to new life, full of glory. Jesus says, "Behold, I am making all things new" (Revelation 21:5).

Flowing from the cross, God's forgiveness, love, and power transform our lives. He wants to put splendour where there was shame, life where there was death.

Robert Cornwall, brother of celebrated Pentecostal Judson, pastored a small church in Oregon. There was not enough income to live on, so he took a job one day a week at a local hospital as a counsellor. On the first day he clocked in, he was led across the hospital to a ward they simply called "Room 37". The door was opened, Cornwall was led in and told they would return for him in one hour. Inside were thirty-seven psychotic patients, half naked, many wearing nappies for incontinence. They sat on benches around the walls in a psychotic and drug-induced stupor. The floor was covered in excrement. Cornwall tried to communicate with one or two, introducing himself, but got no reaction at all. He saw a small patch of unstained floor space and sat down and was led by the Spirit to begin singing:

> *Yes, Jesus loves me, Yes Jesus loves me,*
> *Yes, Jesus loves me: the Bible tells me so.*

The patients sat and stared but gave no sense of engagement. At the end of the hour the door opened and Cornwall was let out. He returned for the next few weeks and was shown to Room 37, where he did exactly the same, sitting on the floor, singing the same song. There was no conversation, no apparent response, just his singing. But on the fourth visit, as he sat on the floor and began singing, one of the patients came and sat next to him, and began to sing with him. I heard Judson Cornwall claim that after one month thirty-six of the thirty-seven were released to self-help wards, and within one year all but two had left the hospital. Of the thirty-seven, two became members of his church.

Decades on I have no way to verify this story – both Judson Cornwall, who I heard tell the story, and his brother Robert have passed away. But the detail that only two of the thirty-seven became members of the church makes me inclined to believe it – no instant revival, and the whole hospital didn't come to faith. But a few lives were changed by the tender witness of a Christian who sang of the Saviour's love. It's just the sort of thing Jesus would do. It's just the sort of place Jesus would send his church. Restoring the ruined to splendour.

God is ever the God who says that he will "restore the splendour of Jacob like the splendour of Israel, though destroyers have laid them waste and have ruined their vines" (Nahum 2:2 NIV). He is the God who restores. And we who love God, who follow his Son Jesus and are filled with his Spirit, will also be led to restore the splendour of lives and lands which have been plundered, emptied and ruined. It's what God does.

Chapter 14

Mercy Me

"The quality of mercy is not strained. It droppeth as the gentle rain from heaven upon the place beneath. It is twice blessed. It blesseth him that gives and him that takes." [59]

William Shakespeare

In Graham Green's *Brighton Rock* the priest is discussing with Pinkie what will happen to a man who has lived a rotten life and then committed suicide. He says, "You cannot conceive, my child, nor can I or anyone, the appalling strangeness of the mercy of God."[60] God's mercy is an alien mercy. It comes to us undeserved and unexpected. And it is a wide mercy, wide enough to make even the foulest clean. In the New Testament Jude describes the Christian as one who is "waiting for the mercy of our Lord Jesus Christ that leads to eternal life" (Jude 21). This is the state, the standing of the Christian who is looking for the coming of Christ bringing salvation. This spiritually upward gaze is coupled with a globally outward focus as we engage in mercy mission. As we wait to receive mercy for ourselves, we live to give mercy to others. Mercy is the hallmark of Christ and of all true Christians, and Jesus commanded us: "Be merciful, even as your Father is merciful" (Luke 6:36).

The term Jude uses for mercy is *eleos* which conveys the sense of "compassion, pity, clemency". If grace is getting what

59 Portia in *The Merchant of Venice*, Act IV, Scene 1.
60 Graham Greene, *Brighton Rock*, p. 268.

we do not deserve (by way of gifts) then mercy is not getting what we do deserve. We are spared our just desserts, divine justice in the form of punishment for our sins.

God's mercy triumphs over God's justice at the cross where the psalmist says: "Mercy and truth are met together; righteousness and peace have kissed each other" (Psalm 85:10 KJV). There is a wideness in God's mercy who "does not deal with us according to our sins, nor repay us according to our iniquities" (Psalm 103:10).

I once preached at a conference when, unscripted, I said that God is so full of grace and mercy that he steps into the cesspits of our life and cleans up the vomit we have covered ourselves in. Some folk winced at the metaphor, and one person formally complained about my inappropriate and vulgar language.

A couple of weeks later I received a letter from a lady who said she had been struggling with her faith and had reached the point of giving up on it and returning to the world. However, she wrote to say my vulgar illustration had powerfully and prophetically reminded her of God's great mercy to her in the past and was in fact a word of mercy reaching to her in her present state. She explained that she had been brought up in a devout and strict Christian home. She had met the Lord when she was a teenager but, as the reins came off at university, she backslid hard and fast into a life marked by partying, sex, and booze.

One night she was out in a taxi. She had already consumed a half-bottle of vodka, and a wave of drunken nausea hit her. Stopping the taxi, she opened the door and begun vomiting violently. There, in the vomit of her life, from deep within, she came to her senses and cried out to God for mercy. Immediately she was filled with the Holy Spirit and began singing in tongues. She wrote that her pagan boyfriend and taxi driver were utterly freaked – one minute dazed, drunk, and vomiting; the next, sober, but drunk on the Spirit, singing worship in an unknown language. Mercy came to the rescue in the vomit. She wrote to tell me that, years later, about to give up on her faith, my reference in the sermon to God meeting us in the vomit of our lives was her testimony, and that God was reminding her of his mercy, and again extending mercy so that she would not turn her back on him.

It is this mercy – real, visceral, life-changing mercy – which Jude calls the church to demonstrate!

1. Tender truth-tellers

"Have mercy on those who doubt" (Jude 22).

The church Jude writes to has been defiled by false teachers who have undermined the gospel and eroded the faith once delivered. Its members have been taken in. They don't know what to believe any more, and they are wavering in doubt. The Greek here is *diakrino*, literally meaning "split judgment". They are torn between the apostolic gospel and the new gospel. While Jude has ferocious things to say about the false teachers, and in fact the bulk of his message is a direct, untempered attack on them, yet his tone is merciful and gracious to the wandering flock that are, in part, victims and must not be subjected to further persecution. Jude does not accuse them, or judge them. He does not belittle them or berate them.

The sheep have strayed from sound doctrine, but Jude, like a good shepherd, wants to bring them back to the fold rather than leave them to the wolves. He calls those who are true to the apostolic faith not to move away from those who are wobbling, but to move toward them and show mercy. Jude is certainly not compromising on doctrine – he has urged the church to "contend for the faith that was once for all delivered" (verse 3). But Christians are not truth police, and the church is not the Grand Inquisition. Divine mercy is no mere liberal all-embracing, all-inclusive tolerance. Mercy is a tender heart wooing back those eating thistles, to the green pasture and calm waters of the gospel.

Surely those deviating or wobbling are more likely to respond and listen to sound doctrine if it comes from a gracious, compassionate heart than a ranting, accusing, condemning spirit. At times when Christians "stray from the truth" as we perceive it, we can be quick to judge, to separate and condemn. One major thread in the history of the church is division, with its condemnation of those we disagree with. It was ever thus – just read the New Testament epistles and see the power struggles behind them.

In 1054 the church opened up a rift between East and West – and the Catholics and the Orthodox barely spoke or acknowledged each other again for nearly a thousand years. Karl Barth and Emil Brunner were theologians, friends, and colleagues in the 1920s, uniting in their challenge and correction of German liberal theology. Sadly, in the early 1930s they fell out over the issue of whether we can know God through creation and conscience. Brunner said a qualified yes, but Barth wrote a scathing booklet against Brunner called *Nein* ("No"). Barth got nasty, and said Brunner was a snake needing striking before it mesmerized you then struck and poisoned you! Brunner was more gracious and for years tried to keep dialogue open, but Barth went silent, refusing even to acknowledge Brunner, who retreated into his rejection and self-justification while Barth went on to dominate theology for decades.

Thirty years later a former doctoral student of both professors, Peter Vogelsanger, went to Barth as Brunner lay on his deathbed in an attempt to broker a reconciliation. Barth was ill but dictated a note saying:

> *If he is alive and it is possible, tell him I commend him to OUR God. And tell him the time when I thought I should*

say no to him is long since past and that we all live only by the fact that a great and **merciful** *God speaks his gracious YES to all of us.*

Dr Vogelsanger managed to deliver the message. He records that Brunner smiled, fell into a coma, and shortly after died. Barth's word of God's merciful *yes* were the last Brunner heard, healing thirty years of the cursed *no* over his life, and ushering him into the presence of God with a *yes*.[61]

Truth without mercy is almost as unchristian as mercy without truth. Let us be those who preach a gospel of God's great mercy with mercy.

2. Fearless firemen

"Save others by snatching them out of the fire" (Jude 23a).

Jude calls the church to save people from the fire of death and hell. Mercy is not a sentimental feeling; it involves action. The greatest act of mercy I can do is to save someone from eternal fire. Jesus' death and resurrection are the means of purchasing our salvation. Peter states: "There is salvation in no one else, for there no other name under heaven given among men by which we must be saved" (Acts 4:12). The church is the community of the saved and the community of salvation, preaching to the nations that, "whoever believes and is baptized will be saved, whoever does not believe will be condemned" (Mark 16:15–16). The early Church Fathers said simply *extra ecclesiam nulla salus* – "outside the church there is no salvation". They conceived of the church as Noah's ark, God's mercy ship, wrestling with the waves of sin, dissipation and judgment, reaching overboard to rescue the drowning.

---

61 A portion of the 4 April 1966, letter from Barth to Peter Vogelsanger is quoted in Eberhard Busch, *Karl Barth: His Life from Letters and Autobiographical Texts*, pp. 476–77.

Salvation is "for" God, "unto" eternal life and "from" the fire. This is not a popular theme in today's church but it is a biblical one. That alone makes sense of the holiness of God, the necessity for sacrifice at Calvary, and the urgency of the Great Commission. The gospel is the mercy of salvation, from a fate worse than death. John's vision of the world's end, the general resurrection, and the last judgment depicts the demonic and the unrighteous being thrown in a lake of fire and brimstone (Revelation 21:8). Whatever this image figures, and some think they are merely metaphorical or figurative, words cannot bear a greater weight than the terrible reality to which they point. Hell must be of greater and more awful, terror-full reality than the metaphor presents. We must not miss the point here: there is a hell, and we sinners deserve hell, but God's mercy interferes, God's mercy intervenes.

If we reject Scripture and refuse to believe in a judging God and eternal hell, then the gospel, the cross, and the mission of the church lose all meaning. Without the doctrine of judgment and eternal hell from which to save people through believing in the gospel of Christ, the church becomes little more than a group of ill-trained social workers. Let's be honest, if we do not believe in God's warning of judgment day and punishment in hell, we definitely do not need a substitutionary atonement by the only perfect man, the Son of God. And if we do not believe that people are lost in sin and need to be saved, then we need not engage in mission or evangelism. Do we even need the church? This has often been the way of the liberal church in all her incarnations. I read one emergent liberal church leader who wrote: "Evangelism or mission for me is no longer persuading people to believe what I believe, it is more about shared experiences and encounters."

What utter tosh. Paul said that "knowing the *fear* of the Lord, we persuade others" (2 Corinthians 5:11 italics mine). If, as Jesus and the apostles believed and taught, men and women are lost and need rescuing, then having little trysts with shared experiences and shared encounters is as much use as a trap door on a lifeboat. Mission is mercy. The former Eton, Cambridge, and England cricket captain, C. T. Studd, had a revelation of the gospel, of what was truly at stake, and of what the church was here for. Forsaking fame and fortune to be a missionary in China, then India, and finally Africa, he gave this testimony: "Some want to live within the sound of church or chapel bells. I want to run a rescue shop within a yard of hell."

And whom does Jude say we should save? I think it is the very false teachers corrupting his church! Earlier he has spoken of the eternal fire of judgment (verses 7–8) symbolized by the destruction of Sodom and Gomorrah that awaits the false teachers who are guilty of gross sin. And yet, amazingly, the very people who have defiled and demonized the church are those whom Jude calls the church to save from the flames. Jude wants the church members, who have been betrayed and abused by these imposing false apostles, to show mercy and grace to them.

There is a story of a remarkable incident of mercy in the First World War. A German soldier was wounded and taken captive. An English officer and medical orderly inspected him and the officer said, "Look after him and give him a drink." As he walked away the German soldier reached for a pistol and shot at the British officer, fortunately missing. The officer could have executed the German prisoner there and then. Instead he looked at the orderly and said, "Look after him all the same." That's mercy. That's Jesus who prayed for those who slayed him – Father forgive them! That's Paul who, having been taken outside the city, stoned and left for dead, gets up miraculously, and immediately re-enters the city to witness again, and hold out the gospel of life to those who had just stoned him (Acts 14:20).

3. Hating sin yet deeply loving the sinner

"To others show mercy with fear, hating even the garment stained by the flesh" (Jude 1:23b).

The final categories of people who are to receive mercy are those who are *morally* fallen – those whose very garments are soiled by sin. Jude uses the Greek word *chiton* which referred to an undergarment next to the skin, which he describes as soiled by the *sarx*, the base fleshly nature. The false teachers have turned the gospel of grace into sensuality (verse 4), and their mark is sexual immorality and unnatural desire (verse 7), defiled flesh (verse 8) and ungodly passions (verse 18). To *these* people – these immoral, unclean, defiled people – Jude says show radical mercy! Without compromising on their own moral purity, *fearing judgment and hating sin,* they are to embrace sinners with tender mercy. Intolerance of sin is not intolerance of sinners. We are to love the sinner while loathing the sin.

Some say this cliché, credited actually to Gandhi, is impossible, yet as a parent of testosterone-filled young men I know it is not. Liberals sometimes accept the sin because they accept the sinner. Evangelicals sometimes reject the sinner because of their hatred of sin. But Jude exhorts us to neither condone sin nor condemn sinners. Paul said: "If anyone is caught in any transgression, you who are spiritual should restore him in a spirit of gentleness. Keep watch on yourself, lest you too be tempted" (Galatians 6:1).

Shawn O'Donnell writes a clever and challenging pro-gay blog in which he has suggested the oft spouted thought of "love the sinner and hate the sin" is actually just shorthand for "hate the sinner"! He provokes the church: "Show me your love – where is it?" Now, O'Donnell's point of reference as to what love is needs teasing out. I suspect what he means by love is total acceptance of a lifestyle the Bible does not condone. The Bible is clear that we must love God, that to love God is to obey his commandments, and that to warn people of divine judgment on sin is the most loving thing we can do. But what O'Donnell is saying to us, and what I believe we must heed, is that his experience of church has been harsh, rejecting, and devoid of love.

I personally believe that homophobia is more sinful than homosexuality. It is a form of hatred, whereas homosexuality is a misdirected longing for love. I recall watching a BBC 2 Louis Theroux documentary on a church whose mission has been to parade outside gay events, even funerals for homosexuals, and rage at them with indecent, mocking placards, calling down curses in the most aggressive way. This is not prophetic, this is not Christ-like. Let us be truth-tellers… with mercy. Paul exhorts us always to be "speaking the truth in love" (Ephesians 4:15). We must robustly defend biblical truth and biblical ethics, but we do so with grace and mercy for those we speak to, and humility and fear for ourselves, not forgetting as Jude reminds us that we too are those awaiting the mercy of God coming in Christ (verse 21). It really is possible to love the sinner and hate the sin, when we recognize that we ourselves are sinners who are nevertheless loved by God.

Jesus, of course, embodied this tension. In the mesmerizing passage at the beginning of John 8, the mercy of God is so scandalous that some early manuscripts cut it out, embarrassed by grace. Here the Pharisees catch a woman in the act of adultery (how ever did they manage that?). Adultery was a moral crime punishable by stoning according to Mosaic law. They push this woman in front of Jesus (where was the man?) to see if he will uphold the law. This test is a trap, but it is based on their knowing his mercy and expecting him not to stone her. Then he can be accused of being a law-breaker himself.

Rather than play their game of yes or no, Jesus suggests we give the first stone to the man without sin. They all leave, the oldest with the longest list of sins going first. When Jesus asks the woman if anyone has condemned her, she replies in relief and amazement, "No one, Lord." Jesus loves the sinner – "Neither do I condemn you" – and hates the sin – "go, and from now on sin no more."

Pre-eminently Jesus' death at Calvary was an act wherein God showed he hated sin (the cross is punishment for sin) and yet loved sinners (the cross is atonement for sinners). At the cross, justice and mercy kiss. Justice that must punish sin, mercy that pays for sin.

And as we proclaim the good news of this God who died for us at Calvary, we become the bringers of mercy, holding out the mercy of God that saves to the uttermost. Jesus said, "Blessed are the merciful, for they shall receive mercy" (Matthew 5:7).

Chapter 15
Snobs, Dogs, and Flags

The true definition of a snob is one who craves for what separates men rather than unites them.[62]
John Buchan

A vicar friend took his worship team to a "worship event". On arriving he was met by a person who asked, "Are you a VIP?" Somewhat bemused he replied, "I fear by your definition we may not be VIPs…" The smiling attendant responded, "Do you have a VIP ticket?" My friend shook his head. "No, I have just come to worship with my worship group." He was then informed that he would have to buy a standard £9 ticket but could only stand at the back, as the seats at the front were reserved for the VIPs. That's not unreasonable, surely: VIPs sit at the front and non-VIPs stand at the back. After all, VIPs cannot sit with non-VIPs. It just wouldn't be right! Would it?

Two millennia ago James wrote these words:

For if a man comes into your assembly with a gold ring and dressed in fine clothes, and there also comes in a poor man in dirty clothes, and you pay special attention to the one who is wearing the fine clothes, and say, "You sit here in a good place," and you say to the poor man, "You stand over there, or sit down by my footstool," have you not made distinctions among yourselves, and become judges with evil motives?
James 2:2–4 NASB

---

62 *Pilgrim's Way*, p. 241.

The letter of James is a "re-evaluation of values". James makes us look at things differently, at people differently; he makes us look through God's eyes. And God snubs snobs. Yes, God looks down his nose at them. In James 2 we are asked to re-evaluate our attitudes toward the rich and the poor. In particular James rebukes those who look up to the wealthy and powerful and at the same time look down on the poor and insignificant. James inverts this, suggesting that often the poor are our role models of faith, while the rich are too often role models of abuse.

The American prophet, Francis Chan, once remarked to me, when I pressed him on his own radical lifestyle and his decision to live in material simplicity: "The lifestyle of the majority of Christians in America is identical to the lifestyle of the non-Christians in America." His experience was that the average evangelical had a professed belief which had not influenced their aspirations, appetites, or actions in any noticeable way. The church's values were essentially identical to the world's. Tragic.

There are snobs among the saints

James 2:1–12 tells us that the church is making a distinction between the poor and the rich, the weak and the powerful. There is a preferential bias toward the one who has, over the one who has not. James says that if a rich man comes into the assembly who is evidently *somebody* because he is wearing a gold ring and fine clothing,[63] the church immediately gives him a good place, whereas a poor man in shabby clothing gets to "stand over there" or sit on the floor.

I am reminded of the poignant scene in the 1970s classic comedy *Fawlty Towers*, when a certain Lord Melbury comes to stay at the ill-fated hotel. John Cleese plays Basil Fawlty, the

---

63 Both were symbols of wealth, a signet ring being a symbol of office worn by Roman magistrates, knights and, later on, bishops…

snobby proprietor, who gets all giddy at "top drawer" clientele. One meal time he turfs out of the window seat a harmless middle-class family in order to give Lord Melbury the sea-view seat, fawning over nobility and not worrying about offending the lower-classed family. The irony is that Lord Melbury turns out to be no aristocrat at all. He is a petty con-man and thief who is eventually arrested by another hotel guest who turns out to be an undercover policeman – one whom Basil Fawlty had previously scorned because of his working class accent! The drama ends with Basil shouting at a true peer of the realm, who chooses not to stay at Fawlty Towers, "You snobs!" But of course it is Basil who is the snob. And sadly it is the church that so often proves to be a religious version of snobbish Fawlty Towers, looking down on some and up to others.

In fact many Christians fall into a sort of religious snobbery: *evangelical* snobs can think they are better because of their sound doctrine; *Pentecostal* snobs can feel themselves superior because they are charismatic; *Anglo-Catholic* snobs may think they are superior because of their aesthetics; *liberal* snobs can think they are better because of their inclusive ethics; *emergent* snobs can think they are better because of their religious pragmatics.

Many Christians just fall for the age-old snobberies: *intellectual* snobs pride themselves on going to public school, or top flight Ivy League/Oxbridge universities, or getting first-class or higher level degrees; *material* snobs pride themselves on their wealth, house, possessions, holidays; *fashionable* snobs pride themselves on keeping up with the latest look, accessories, hair styling, music... *racial* snobs pride themselves on being English or White or American or Arab or Italian or anything which makes them think their race gives them a superiority over others. The famed Oxford academic, C. S. Lewis, said that before he became a Christian he was a *chronological* snob,[64] rejecting the

---

64 C. S. Lewis, *Surprised by Joy*, pp. 207–208.

Bible because it was full of the old-fashioned ideas that he had grown up with and grown away from.

Oxford, where I live, is one of the grandest and most distinguished cities in Britain, and famous the world over for its ancient university, impressive architecture, and as a seat of learning and power. It is also a place dripping with snobbery, a snobbery that has seeped into the church. I wonder what James 2 has to say to the class-conscious mother who rang up our church and said her daughter was coming to Oxford University and would we make sure she got in with the "right sort" – not at all meaning a Christian community, but the upper-class students. I wonder what James 2 has to say to those Christian house-parties which are run exclusively for the top public school attendees? I wonder what James 2 has to say to the chaplain who invited me to speak at their college chapel, and when asked by a tutor whether the chaplain and I had met as undergraduates, the chaplain replied, "No, when I was at Oxford, he was in trade…" To even use such archaic social categories as "trade" and "professional" betrays a spirit of classism and snobbery. This chaplain sneered at the fact I had earned a living with my hands; I commented that I followed a carpenter who was also in trade!

Or what would James say to the Oxford undergraduate who, when I was a chaplain, once asked me why I pretended I went to Oxford. Surprised, I enquired how I gave the impression that I was impersonating Oxford graduates. She replied, "By using long words in sermons" – as if long words were the preserve only of Oxford students! And then there was the undergraduate who once commented on my clothing: "Why are you wearing a pink shirt – you aren't posh!" – as if only the upper middle classes were allowed such kit.

All these little examples, which have lodged amusingly in my memory, reflect a deep-seated snobbery, and no doubt those students would be shocked to hear themselves many years later.

I am aware that some might read the last paragraph and think that I am an inverted snob with a chip on my shoulder. Perhaps I am. But when I read the Gospels and the epistles I see no basis for the élitism that I have experienced for decades in the church. Where is the shame in my own Anglican denomination where, until Victorian times, the wealthy and landed paid for boxed pews and sat at the front of churches often on raised plinths, while the poor sat at the back on benches? Had they not read James 2?! Until after the Second World War in England it was virtually impossible to be ordained without being a graduate of Oxford or Cambridge. Thank God that the times, they are a changing – slowly.

The church should be the most egalitarian community in the world, for here there is neither Jew nor Greek, slave nor free, male nor female, but all are one in Christ (Galatians 3:28). There is only level ground at the foot of the cross. There we all stand, or kneel, pitiful, blind, naked, wretched, sinners dependent on the handout of grace. At Pentecost the Spirit was given to sons and daughters, servants and free, old and young. The age of the Spirit is the age of divine egalitarianism. The church should apply the Spirit level, for he is a Leveller. The Spirit has always united what society has divided. When the Spirit fell on Azusa Street in 1906, birthing the Pentecostal revival, outsiders complained that Black sons of slaves sat together with White middle-class ladies. Hallelujah! The Spirit baptizes us into one body.

Snobbery is robbery

Snobbery robs the snob and the one snobbed. James uses the Greek word *atimazo* (verse 6) meaning "to despise, dishonour, demean, treat shamefully". The action of distinguishing between rich and poor, and elevating the rich over the poor in the church, is to rob the poor of honour and esteem and worth. Also snobbery is robbery for the snob, because it backfires, robbing the snob of blessing. The snob is robbed because, by looking down on the poor, he cannot learn from them, he cannot receive from them and also does not learn to live by faith in God. So often the poor, having little, have learned to lean on God. They understand the deep things of God. To ignore the poor is often to cut oneself off from men and women of true faith.

There is an ugly pseudo-Pentecostal doctrine that God blesses in every area of life, including materially, and therefore to be poor is indicative of being cursed; conversely the rich and powerful are somehow divinely blessed. James suggests the opposite (2:5). The people of faith tend to be the poor who have learned about God by leaning on him and not relying on their wealth. Jesus acutely observed how difficult it is for a rich man to enter the kingdom of heaven, precisely because money insulates them against dependency and faith in Christ. The wealthy often have faith in wealth not God. James says that the self-reliant, those who are independently wealthy, are in danger of being blasphemers and abusers. Snobbery robs the snob; the irony is that the snob thinks he is gaining something by associating or sucking up to one group and dissociating from another. But in fact the opposite is true.

The snob has no authentic faith

James argues that the person of faith must not be a person of partiality. His argument continues that faith is proved by good works (2:14–26), so where there is clear favouritism, authentic faith is called into question. The Swiss theologian Karl Barth termed the great gulf between God and humankind as the "infinite qualitative distinction".[65] Jesus, as Lord God, may rightly literally look down on everyone. Jesus is the only man born of

---

65 Karl Barth, *The Epistle to the Romans*, pp. 10. 355, 356.

woman who has the right to be a snob. Yet, quite to the contrary, in his *incarnation* Jesus takes the form of a slave, born not into the noblest royal family but to a humble carpenter, to grow up in a backwater called Nazareth. In his *associations* Jesus is friend to tax collectors and sinners, a major reason he was despised and rejected by the social élite of the Sanhedrin, while "the common people heard him gladly" (Mark 12:37 KJV). In his *crucifixion* Jesus was "numbered with the transgressors" (Isaiah 53:12); he was crucified alongside sinners and crucified for sinners. In his *affections* God so loved the world – not just the wealthy, not simply the winners, but all the world. To be a disciple of Christ is to know oneself a saved sinner whose own sins crushed Jesus on the cross. What right have we to think we are somebody, that others are nobodies? We must not be enamoured by anyone of wealth or power or position, for that person too caused Christ to be accursed.

The snob breaks God's law

James says that the royal law is to love your neighbour as yourself (James 2:8–11). How can we fulfil this mandate if we differentiate? To show favouritism is to break the royal law, and if you break this law you break all laws. Make no mistake, snobbery is sin. It is a failure to love your neighbour. It is a violation of the greatest commandment, as Jesus gave it. And strikingly, James specifically lists adultery and murder in the catalogue as comparable with favouritism. Most people who look down their nose at the poor, or uneducated, or unfashionable or… probably wouldn't group themselves with murderers and adulterers; but James does. God does: "law-breakers!"

The snob incurs God's wrath

James 2:13 says that judgment without mercy will be shown to anyone who has shown no mercy. The friend of the poor is the friend of God. Snobbery actually puts you at odds with the most significant person in the universe. Those who think they are a Cut-Above will be Cut Down to size. Those who think they are part of the In crowd will be left Out. God snubs snobs. He does not look on outward appearance but on the heart (1 Samuel 16:7), opposing the proud but giving grace to the humble (James 4:6).

The snob misplaces pride

There is something to be truly proud of. James offers two antidotes to snobbery, two principles which are the basis of true pride. First: all members of the church are family; and second, true glory is found by associating with Christ the Lord of glory, not with the noble or powerful of this world.

Throughout the letter of James, but poignantly in chapter 2 when addressing this issue, James refers to his readers as "brothers" (verses 1, 5, and 14, which according to ancient custom included sisters too). In the midst of challenging distinctions and favouritism, James keeps reminding them they are first and foremost family, brothers and sisters in Jesus Christ. They are sons and daughters of the same heavenly Father. *Fraternité* means *egalité*. Financial, social, intellectual, racial differences are irrelevant in Christ. What unites Christians is blood ties – Christ's blood – born again from the same heavenly womb by the Spirit. That shared experience, shared paternity, shared birth, shared DNA, will allow for no sibling rivalry or snobbery.

I recall visiting my dad who, after many years, had finally finished researching our family tree. He was thrilled to show me all our ancestors, including some nobles and distinguished lords. In one Cornish village each year on a festival day a game is played, where young men run through the street chasing a silver ball and shouting our family motto, in commemoration of an ancestor, a feudal lord who raised an army to fight against the English – where he duly lost! My dad proudly pointed out a Quaker ancestor, nicely named Charity Pepper, who sailed with William Penn to America.

Then Dad's voice hushed and his brow furrowed, as he said, "I've something to show you that will upset you." Oh no – what deep dark secret lay buried in the family vaults? What shame was about to be exposed? Dad pointed to a photocopy of a Victorian document, his nail tapping the print, pointing out a large letter X. Next to this X were written the words: "This is the mark of…" I looked at my father and said, "So someone couldn't write their name?" and he whispered, with head bowed, "Yes, your great-great-grandmother was an illiterate." I laughed out loud. My ancestors: lords, ladies and illiterates. Perfect! The novelist Alexander Theroux once wrote: "Snobbery is about the problem of belonging."

We must learn to take pride in what is truly glorious. James writes about our shared "faith in our Lord Jesus Christ, the Lord of glory" (James 2:1). The Greek is awkward but best translated as "faith in the Lord Jesus Christ our glory". True glory is not what we have achieved but what we receive as a gift from Christ. It is glory by association – Christ is our glory, he is the lifter of our heads. We so often glory in what tarnishes: academic success, material possessions, good looks, family pedigree, religious experiences. These things are not wrong in and of themselves, and some may even be virtuous. But they must lead us to look up to God in gratitude, never down on others with attitude. Everyone – the powerful and the pauper – has sinned and fallen short of God's glory (Romans 3:23); and yet on all who receive Christ that glory is restored, as with unveiled faces, beholding the glory of the Lord, we are being transformed from one degree of glory into his likeness, by the Spirit (2 Corinthians 3:18).

Flags and dogs

I think I have learned more about this whole theme from my colleagues Charlie and Anita Cleverly than anyone else. Two things in particular stand out, which I am calling flags and dogs: their commitment and heart for the nations; and their love and service to the poor, the outsider, the marginalized. Both of these have exposed my sin and snobbery.

Flags

I confess I've always leaned toward being a xenophobic snob. I have been so proud of being an Englishman and of English history that I regarded the English as the most superior race among humankind, blessed of God, with the greatest empire, greatest contribution to civilization, greatest armies, and so on. Regardless of whether such claims could be substantiated by history, I held to this very deeply, and inadvertently looked down on all other nations as somehow inferior. I never tried hard to learn foreign languages (despite doing French, German, and Spanish at school) because I felt "the foreigners" ought to learn English!

When Charlie and Anita named our church motto as "a house of prayer for all nations" I rather protested, "So you want us to pray for foreigners then?" When they bought a collection of national flags on poles and placed them prominently in the church, I thought it vulgar and inappropriate. When they regularly publicly acknowledged visiting foreigners in the congregation and even invited some to preach, and, worse still, even employed a few foreigners on the staff team, I cannot tell you how uncomfortable I found it all. Deep resentments, deep racisms, rumbled in my soul. But slowly, and painfully, God began to melt my ice-hard heart. I realized much of my racism and xenophobia came from sheer ignorance – I actually had no foreign friends, and didn't really know anyone who was of a different nationality. By actually meeting people from other countries, and spending time with them, and receiving care, kindness, prayers, and encouragement from them, my heart began to melt.

I had an Indian intern whose love for Christ, humility, servant heart and costly following of Christ exposed my own half-hearted commitment. I got to know a Korean who was powerfully used by God in mission. He loved me and insisted on paying for my post-graduate research. I met with a wonderful German woman whose inspirational walk with God, and words of life spoken into my life, transformed my attitude of deep-seated resentment to Germany for two world wars. I worked with a Frenchman who humbled me by his passion and effectiveness in reaching the nations who were coming as graduate students to Oxford and who filled our church meeting rooms with language schools, national parties, and the smell of foreign cuisine. I worked with a giant Austrian whose brilliance in theology was overshadowed only by his connection with God in prayer, and who told me he wanted to learn Serbo-Croat so he could engage with the growing Serbian community in his native country. I'm humbled by this holy man and honoured to know him. I got to know a Ugandan, who had suffered attempted assassination when he converted from Islam to Christianity, and who energetically seeks to communicate Christ with his former Muslim brothers. I met an extraordinary Indian family who welcomed me into their home, showered me with gifts and love and, when I was hospitalized and incapacitated for months, cared for me more than any others. They won me for India! I was given administrative support from a Polish woman who proved to be exceptional at everything.

Meeting, knowing, receiving from, worshipping with, serving alongside people of different races, creeds, and colours, has caused a personal revolution in my life. It is amazing and shocking that I could have been a Christian for years, a minister for years, but have such large tracts of my life held by sin and the flesh. My groundless nationalistic pride and xenophobia dissipated. Foreign accents and different skin colours no longer evoked a deeply seated disdain. Instead they elicited a sense of anticipation, that as I got to know these folk I was to receive and learn and grow more human and more like Christ.

Dogs

One day, just before a service, a churchwarden came to me when I was standing with Charlie Cleverly and said that a man had come into church with his small dog and what would we like done, if anything. The warden did not think the dog was a problem but wanted our advice. I instinctively said, "Get rid of it, no dogs in church." But Charlie said, "No, let him stay, I love the smell of dogs in church." I could barely contain myself – a flea-ridden dog in church! But his owner was a homeless guy, and he stayed well beyond the service. Jim became a regular church member, got baptized with great joy and with a church crowded with people from the street – those "from the other side of town" whom Jim had touched and blessed. Jim and his dog became my friends. So I was profoundly moved one day when he asked me if I would take ownership of his dog, if ever he had to move on. I still have the copy of Milton's *Paradise Lost* which he bought me. He occasionally passes through Oxford on walkabout; and whenever he does, he stops by, with some hand-picked wild flowers or fruits, and we drink tea, and he tells me about God at work. And I am humbled.

Who do you want in church? If you want God, perhaps you need to have flags and dogs.

What Do You Want to Do Next?

This book has been about seeing differently and being different and making a difference. I hope it has conveyed something of God's heart to your heart for justice and mercy, and nudged you further in being a doer as well as a hearer of the word. Far be it from me to make you feel guilty; rather, I wrote this to inspire you to the thrill of the chase of being Christ-like. I have sought to open up the Bible's themes, and see if together we couldn't be better hearers and doers. Godliness – and not guilt – must be our motivation – compassion not condemnation.

Actually I suspect that condemnation doesn't work for very long. Those induced to acts of justice and mercy through guilt are not likely to sustain their giving and serving. Once the guilt diminishes, they are on to something else. Some are motivated to works of justice and mercy by a selfish altruism,[66] where their good works are done to make them feel good about themselves. Better than nothing, for at least something is done, and someone benefits, but surely there must be a better motivator.

My prayer for you is that, enlightened by God's word and moved with his compassion, you will seek his kingdom and the righteousness – the justice – that comes with it.

God bless you… to go bless others.

---

66 Tony Vaux, *The Selfish Altruist* – a remarkable book by a former Oxfam emergency manager who spent twenty years exploring the motivations of relief workers.

Bibliography

Barth, K., *The Epistle to the Romans*, Oxford: Oxford University Press, 1968.

Bauer, W., Arndt, W. F. & Gingrich, F. W., *A Greek–English Lexicon of the New Testament and Other Early Christian Literature*. Chicago: University of Chicago Press, 1979.

Brown, C. (ed.), *New International Dictionary of New Testament Theology: Vol. 3*. Grand Rapids, MI: Eerdmans, 1986.

Buchan, J., *Pilgrim's Way: An Essay in Recollection*, New York, NY: Carrol & Graff, 1984 (first published 1940).

Busch, E., *Karl Barth: His Life from Letters and Autobiographical Texts* (trans. by Bowden, J.), Philadelphia, PA: Fortress, 1976.

Capon, R. F., *Between Noon and Three*, San Francisco, CA: Harper and Row, 1982.

Cowper, W., "For the Poor" from *The Works of William Cowper*, Charleston, SC: BiblioBazaar, 2010.

Dawkins R., *River out of Eden: A Darwinian View of Life*, London: Phoenix, 1996.

Dostoyevsky, F., *Crime and Punishment*, London: Penguin Classics, 2003.

Exell, J. (ed.), *The Biblical Illustrator*, 1887.

Finney, C. G., *Letters On Revivals: No. 23*, 21 January 1846 (retrieved June 2011 from http://www.gospeltruth.net/1846OE/46_lets_art/460121_let_on_revival_23.htm).

Forster, E. M., *A Passage to India*, London: Penguin Classics, 2005.

Forsyth, P. T., *Missions in State and Church: Sermons and Addresses*, London: Hodder & Stoughton, 1908.

Gandhi, M. K. (1983). *An Autobiography: The Story of My Experiments with Truth*, New York, NY: Dover Publications.

Garff, J., *Søren Kierkegaard: A Biography*, Princeton, NJ: Princeton University Press, 2007.

Greene, G., *Brighton Rock,* London: Vintage, 2002.

Heschel, A. J., *The Prophets*, New York, NY: Harper Perennial Modern Classics, 2001.

Hopkins, G. M., "As Kingfishers Catch Fire" in *The Major Works*, Oxford: Oxford University Press, 2009.

Flavius Josephus, *Jewish Antiquities*, Ware: Wordsworth Editions Ltd., 2006.

Lewis, C. S., *Surprised by Joy*, London: Collins, 1998.

Lewis, C. S., *Letters to an American Lady,* Grand Rapids, MI: Eerdmans, 1986.

Lewis, C. S., *The Screwtape Letters*, New York, NY: MacMillan, 1982.

Mandela, N., *Long Walk to Freedom*, London: Abacus, 1995.

Manning, B., *Abba's Child: The Cry of the Heart for Intimate Belonging*, Colorado Springs, CO: Nav Press, 2002.

McGaw, F. A., *Praying Hyde – John Hyde's Prayer Life*, Chicago, IL: Moody Press, 1950.

Mill, J. S., *On Liberty*, Boston: Tricknor and Fields, 1863.

Moore, C., *Provocations: The Spiritual Writings of Kierkegaard*, New York, NY: Orbis Books, 2003.

Nietzsche, F., *Beyond Good and Evil*, London: Penguin Classics, 2003.

Nolland, J., *Luke 1–9:20: Word Biblical Commentary*, Dallas, TX: World Books, 1989.

Oswalt, J., *The Book of Isaiah 40–66: New International Commentary on the Old Testament*, Grand Rapids, MI: Eerdmans, 1998.

Our Daily Bread, Sandside: RBC Ministries, 6 March 1994.

Pascal, B., Section VII, Morality and Doctrine of *Pensées*, London: Penguin Classics, 2003.

Ruskin, J., *The Two Paths*, Teddington: The Echo Library, 2007.

Ruskin, J., *The Seven Lamps of Architecture*, London: Smith & Elder, 1849.

Shakespeare, W., *King Lear* from *The Complete Works*. Oxford: Oxford University Press, 2005.

Shakespeare, W., *The Merchant of Venice*. Oxford: Oxford World Classics, 2008.

Stewart, J. S., *The Heralds of God,* Whitefish, Mt: Kessinger Publishing, 2010.

ten Boom, C. *A Prisoner and Yet,* Washington, DC: CLC Publishers, 1954.

Tolkien, J. R. R., *The Lord of the Rings Trilogy, The Return of the King,* Boston: Houghton Mifflin, 2007.

Vaux, T., *The Selfish Altruist: Relief Work in Famine and War,* Abingdon: Earthscan, 2001.

Voderholzer, R., *Meet Henri de Lubac: His Life and Work,* San Francisco, CA: Ignatius Press, 2008.

Voltaire, F., *Philosophical Dictionary*, New York, NY: Dover Publications, 2010.

Yancey, P., *What's So Amazing About Grace?*, Grand Rapids, MI: Zondervan Publishing House, 1997.

Zacharias, R., *Jesus Among Other Gods: The Absolute Claims of the Christian Message*, Nashville, TN: Thomas Nelson, 2002.

Websites visited

American Rhetoric: Top 100 Speeches, "Martin Luther King, Jr.: 'I have a Dream'", (published online 2011) <http://www.americanrhetoric.com/speeches/mlkihaveadream.htm>, accessed June 2011.

Aquilina, M. A., "Double Take on Early Christianity", (published online 2000) <http://www.catholiceducation.org/articles/history/world/wh0140.htm> accessed June 2011.

Avert, "STD Statistics and STDs in the UK", (published online 2011) <http://www.avert.org/std-statistics-uk.htm>, accessed June 2011.

Bible Society, "The Poverty and Justice Bible", (published online 2008) <http://www.povertyandjusticebible.org/> accessed June 2011.

Bryce, J., Black, R. E., Walker, N., Bhutta, Z. A., Lawn, J. E., Steketee, R. W., "Can the world afford to save the lives of 6 million children each year?", (published online 2005) <http://www.givewell.org/files/Cause1-2/+UNICEF/Lancet%20can_the_world_affort_child_surv.pdf> accessed June 2011.

Crimestoppers, "Latest crime statistics", (published online 2011) <http://www.crimestoppers-uk.org/crime-prevention/latest-crime-statistics> accessed June 2011.

Dawn, M., "Try a Little Tenderness...", (published online 2005) <http://maggidawn.com/try-a-little-tenderness/> accessed June 2011.

Edwards, J., *Sinners in the Hands of an Angry God*, (1741, published online 2007) <http://www.ccel.org/ccel/edwards/sermons.sinners.html> accessed June 2011.

Edwards, J., *Works of Jonathan Edwards: Vol. I, Section: III,* (published online 2005) <http://www.ccel.org/e/edwards/works1.ix.vi.iii.html> accessed June 2011.

Giving What We Can, "It Can Be Solved", (published online 2011) <http://www.givingwhatwecan.org/the-problem/it-can-be-solved.php> accessed June 2011.

Guardian, The, "Oxford to investigate cash-for-places claim", (published online 2002) <www.guardian.co.uk/uk/2002/mar/24/oxbridgeandelitism.highereducation> accessed March 2012.

The Interceders, *The Interceders Encourager No. 20*, (published online 2010) <http://www.calltoprayer.org.uk/encourager20.html> accessed June 2011.

The Judiciary Report, "Bribing a Judge", (published online 2007) <http://www.judiciaryreport.com/bribing_a_judge.htm> accessed June 2011.

King, S., "16 Important Functions of Real Sea Salt", (published online 2010), <http://shawn-king.com/blog/wellnesscoach/1102/16-important-functions-of-real-sea-salt/> accessed June 2011.

Lister, T., "Maps, land and history: Why 1967 still matters", (published online 2011) <http://articles.cnn.com/2011-05-24/world/israel.1967_1_netanya-israeli-forces-syria-and-jordan/2?_s=PM:WORLD> accessed March 2012.

Prison Reform Trust, "Bromley Briefings Prison Factfile", (published online 2011) <http://www.prisonreformtrust.org.uk/

Portals/0/Documents/Fact%20File%20June%202011%20web.pdf>
accessed March 2012.

Ravenhill, L., "Weeping Between the Porch and the Altar: Part 1",
(published online 1994) <http://www.ravenhill.org/weeping1.
htm> accessed June 2011.

Religious Tolerance, "U.S. Divorce Rates for Various Faith Groups,
Age Groups, & Geographic Areas", (published online 2009) <http://
www.religioustolerance.org/chr_dira.htm> accessed June 2011.

Richardson, J., "The Spiritual Roots of our Ecological Crisis – Was
Lynn Wright Right?", (published online 1998) <http://www.
btinternet.com/~j.p.richardson/lynnwhite.html> accessed March
2012.

Steffen, A., "Ending Poverty", (published online 2005) <http://
www.worldchanging.com/archives/001855.html> accessed June
2011.

This is Money, "Best paid jobs: tables of official figures for UK
salaries", (published online 2010) <http://www.thisismoney.
co.uk/money/article-1709280/Best-paid-jobs-A-guide-UK-salaries.
html> accessed June 2011.

Telegraph, The, "Teenage abortions hit record as under 16
pregnancy rate soars" (published online 2009) <http://www.
telegraph.co.uk/health/healthnews/4839713/Teenage-abortions-
hit-record-as-under-16-pregnancy-rate-soars.html> accessed March
2012.

Times, The, (published online 2011) <http://www.timesonline.
co.uk/tol/news/uk/article32258> accessed June 2011.

Why Church, "How many people go to Church in the UK?",
(published online 2011) <http://www.whychurch.org.uk/trends.
php> accessed June 2011.

Wikipedia, "Amazing Grace", (published online 2011) <http://
en.wikipedia.org/wiki/Amazing_Grace> accessed June 2011.

Wordsworth, W., "The Old Cumberland Beggar", (published
online 2009) from <http://rpo.library.utoronto.ca/poem/2353.
html> accessed June 2011.